BEFORE THEIR DIASPORA

A PHOTOGRAPHIC HISTORY OF THE PALESTINIANS 1876–1948

WALID KHALIDI

BEFORE THEIR DIASPORA

BEFORE THEIR DIASPORA

A PHOTOGRAPHIC
HISTORY OF
THE PALESTINIANS
1876–1948

with an introduction and
commentary by

WALID KHALIDI

INSTITUTE FOR PALESTINE STUDIES
WASHINGTON · D.C. · 1984

The Institute for Palestine Studies, founded in Beirut in 1963, is an independent nonprofit Arab research and publication center, which is not affiliated to any political organization or government. The opinions expressed in its publications do not necessarily reflect those of the Institute.

Library of Congress Cataloging in Publication Data

Khalidi, Walid.
  Before their diaspora: a photographic history of the
  Palestinians, 1876–1948.
    1. Palestine—History—1799–1917—Pictorial works.
  2. Palestine—History—1917–1948—Pictorial works.
  3. Israel-Arab War—1948–1949—Pictorial works.
  4. Palestinian Arabs—Pictorial works. I. Institute for
  Palestine Studies (Washington, D.C.) II. Title.
  DS125.K45 1984   956.94′03   84-19821
  ISBN 0-88728-143-5
  ISBN 0-88728-144-3 (pbk.)

Designed by Richard Zonghi

Printed in the United States of America
by Thomas Todd Company, Boston, Massachusetts

To Hassib

CONTENTS

PATRONS

The production of this book was made possible through the generous patronage of Mr. Abdul Majeed Shoman, chairman of the Board of Directors, Arab Bank Ltd., Amman, Jordan; and Mr. Hassib Sabbagh, founder of the Diana Tamari Sabbagh Foundation, Beirut, Lebanon.

SPECIAL ACKNOWLEDGMENTS

MANY individuals and institutions, whom I gratefully list in the preface, helped in completing this volume. But here special mention must be made of the following:

First and foremost my wife, Rasha, who significantly contributed to setting the project on its proper course, and bore the brunt of the effort and time — spread over five difficult years — that I spent on it.

Ms. May Kadi and Prof. Marwan Buheiry, of Beirut, who were intimately involved in the organization of the project from its inception until the summer of 1982, when events and distances separated them from it.

Ms. Kadi meticulously catalogued and supervised the reproduction from the originals of the photographs presented in this book. Through her friends and contacts, she acquired items from private collections and family albums, saving them from obscurity, enriching our selection, and filling in its gaps. She researched the background of many of the photographs, paving the way for their captions to be written. She located relevant collections in different parts of the world and concluded the copyright agreements for the items we printed.

Prof. Buheiry researched and wrote the first draft of the chronology — a considerable task — as well as that of several of the captions. While on a special visit to London, he examined the photographic collection at the Imperial War Museum and made appropriate selections from it.

Mr. Akram Zu'aiter of Amman, orator, essayist, diplomat, retired activist, but above all the walking memory of the Palestinian national movement in the 1930s, who not only made available to us his own unique private collection of photographs, but was indispensable in identifying the personalities, locations, dates, and occasions of many of the photographs we selected.

Ms. Elizabeth Burr, of Cambridge, Massachusetts, who with infinite care and patience scrutinized and edited successive versions of the introductions, chronologies, captions, and preface. Her comments, queries, and suggestions on points of syntax, style, and phraseology were refreshingly pertinent and immensely useful; she was also adept at translating my insular English into continental American. Equally invaluable were her assumption of the complex liaison work with the designer and printer and her firm but always gentle insistence that I meet their deadlines, which largely ensured the successful completion of this project.

Mr. Richard Zonghi, of Boston, Massachusetts, whose clarity of concept, sureness of touch, and prodigious preparatory work are solely responsible for the elegant appearance of this book.

PREFACE

PROTAGONISTS in conflicts are often so obsessed with the history of the conflict in which they have been involved that they are unable to face the emotional and intellectual challenge of transcending the past in order to address the task of achieving a reasonably honorable, if necessarily imperfect, resolution of the conflict. The wronged, or oppressed, party is particularly susceptible to such an obsession.

The intensity and longevity of this obsession is affected by several factors: the nature of the wrong inflicted in the first place, the attitude of third parties to the conflict, and the conduct of the oppressor party after the infliction of the wrong.

For the Palestinians, the oppressed party in their conflict with Zionism, these factors have combined to ensure the prolongation and intensification of their obsession. During the almost seven decades between the early 1880s and 1948, the period covered in this book, the Palestinians were at the receiving end of a Jewish political movement of European provenance, Zionism, which presented them with the deadliest threat, short of physical annihilation, to which a people can be subjected — the denial of their birthright in their ancestral home, Palestine. Nor did this threat remain hypothetical: 1948, the Year of the Catastrophe, as Palestinians call it, witnessed the long-dreaded, inevitable climax of Zionist colonization since the 1880s in the twin phenomena of the establishment of Israel by force of arms in the greater part of Palestine, and the displacement of the Palestinian inhabitants from a score of towns, and from some four hundred villages whose ruined sites became part of the new Jewish state. In the process, at least ten thousand Palestinians were killed and three times that number wounded; 60 percent of the Palestinian population at the time, some 700,000 persons, were rendered homeless. The Palestinians may not have been annihilated in 1948, but they were dispossessed of their country.

World public opinion has been sympathetic to the Palestinians. As erstwhile victims of European colonialism, the Third World countries (including India) have instinctively identified with their cause. The Communist countries (including the USSR and China), while recognizing the existence of Israel, have supported the Palestinians partly because they view their struggle within the context of opposition to Western imperialism, and partly for geopolitical reasons. Important sectors of public opinion in Western Europe have also evinced an understanding of the plight of the Palestinians, reflecting centuries of European association with and sensitivity to the Middle East.

But gratifying as the sympathy of world public opinion has been to the Palestinians, it has been neutralized by the massive support extended to Zionism by the United States both before and after 1948. The United States bears a heavy share of the responsibility, immediately following the end of World War II, for propelling events in Palestine toward their terrible consequences (for the Palestinians) in 1948. American support for Israel since then has steadily escalated despite continued Israeli denial of Palestinian national and human rights. It is American support that above all else has enabled Israel to persist in this denial. What particularly rankles with Palestinians is that the United States' endorsement of their dispossession has been made in the name of the democratic values of American political culture. The irony of this is all the greater because there is evidence to indicate that the majority of the American people would support an evenhanded solution to the Palestinian-Israeli conflict that guaranteed the existence and security of Israel as well as Palestinian national survival and self-determination.

From the beginning of their colonization of Palestine, the architects of the Zionist "dream" excluded from consideration its potential consequences for the Palestinians. The reality of Zionism as translated on the ground was rarely perceived as diverging from the dream, which was (and still is) regarded as pristine; any divergence between the reality and the dream was only a momentary aberration from the dream. Thus the ineluctable link between Zionist action and Palestinian reaction was banished from Zionist consciousness. Since 1948, with the exception of a small Israeli peace movement, the Israelis have succumbed to an emotional and intellectual condition (to which an oppressor is prone) that complements the Palestinians' obsession with the past. This condition is characterized by an acute aversion to a scrutiny, with all its moral implications, of Zionism's historical record in Palestine since the 1880s. So great has their aversion been (and so compelling the apparent psychological need for it) that, with the help of historical revisionism and rationalization, the Israelis have convinced themselves and their supporters either that the Palestinians did not exist at all before 1948, or — if they did — that the Palestinians were the initiators of the conflict and the tormentors of Zion. The Israelis' final refinement of this line of reasoning has been to categorize their Palestinian victims under such rubrics as "fanatics" and "terrorists," the sources of whose behavior must be sought in specious, atavistic fountainheads. Thus have the motives behind Palestinian resistance to Zionism and Israel been traced comfortably *away* from the context of the conflict itself, and equally from those of Israeli introspection and moral responsibility.

If 1948 had marked the end of the impingement of Zionism and Israel on Palestinian rights, Time would still have had a formidable task to heal the wounds already inflicted on the Palestinians.

In fact, throughout the two decades between 1948 and 1967 Israel adamantly refrained from any alleviating gesture of redress or reconciliation, whether in the form of repatriation, repara-

tion, or territorial adjustment. It proceeded, instead, to "legalize" its expropriation of the abandoned movable and immovable properties of the Palestinian refugees and to transfer these properties to Jewish ownership. It imposed military rule on the terrorized Palestinian minority left in its midst. It carried out, in the name of retaliation for the slightest border violations, grossly disproportionate military operations against Palestinian border villages on the Jordanian-controlled West Bank and in the Egyptian-controlled Gaza Strip, villages whose best farmland it had already seized in 1948. It annexed the demilitarized zones and no man's lands on the West Bank. It unilaterally diverted the waters of the Jordan River for its own purposes. It repeatedly flaunted its might by holding military parades in West Jerusalem. During the same two decades, the Palestine problem evolved into the conflict between Israel and the neighboring Arab countries. And in the 1960s Palestinian despair found expression in the concept of armed struggle under the aegis of the Palestine Liberation Organization.

In 1967 Israel went further still. Having wrested the greater part of Palestine in 1948, it was now bent on wresting what land remained in Palestinian hands. Between June and September 1967, it expelled across the Jordan River some 250,000 inmates of the refugee camps located on the West Bank and in the Gaza Strip. It proceeded to apply to the newly occupied territories the very policy of systematic colonization, pursued by the Zionists in Palestine from the 1880s until 1948, that had created the Palestine problem in the first place.

Enjoying an absolute monopoly of power over the Occupied Territories since 1967, Israel has facilitated its colonization of these territories through a whole gamut of administrative, legalistic, economic, psychological, and physical measures. Immediately after the cessation of fighting in June 1967, Israel annexed East Jerusalem and declared the "unified" city its capital. The municipal boundaries were expanded to include large areas of Palestinian territory on the West Bank. Strategic parts of these areas were expropriated and housing projects completed in them to accommodate Jewish settlers "returning home" from Russia and the United States. Bulldozers were dispatched into the Old City of Jerusalem to tear down venerable medieval Muslim religious buildings adjacent to the Wailing Wall. Dozens of Muslim family properties within the Old City walls were seized in the name of "public interest" and transferred to Jewish ownership. Extensive excavations were undertaken next to the foundations of the holiest of Muslim shrines without prior permission of the Muslim religious authorities. Three prosperous villages in the foothills around Latrun were literally erased from the map and their entire population expelled overnight.

The so-called Emergency Regulations, resurrected from the days of British colonial rule, were the cornerstone of Israeli policy. These regulations allowed arrest without warning; censorship of newspapers, books, telegrams, and letters; restriction of movement, limitation of contact with others, dismissal of employees by order of the Minister of Defense, and internal exile and deportation from the country without judicial approval; the opening and closing of areas, the imposition of unlimited curfews, and confiscation and destruction of property. Under the umbrella of these regulations, habeas corpus was routinely denied by the Israeli occupation authorities as was freedom of expression, assembly, and movement. Hundreds of houses were blown up to punish *relatives* of individuals suspected of or involved in resistance. Troops received authorization to fire live ammunition into demonstrations by unarmed civilians, including schoolchildren. Thousands of Palestinians were detained and hundreds subjected to torture in prison. Academic life was disrupted through the periodic suspension of instruction at schools and universities, and the repeated invasion of classrooms and dormitories by special units of the Israeli army. More than one hundred leading citizens (doctors, clergymen, feminists, judges, professors, civil servants, and union leaders) were banished from the country. Elected mayors were dismissed, deported, and (in some cases) maimed with the connivance of Israeli officials. Informers and quislings were subsidized and armed. Israeli colonist vigilantes, armed by their government, were permitted to take the law into their own hands in acts of vandalism and murder.

In the economic field, the Occupied Territories became a hostage market for Israeli products at the expense of local industries. The economic need of Palestinian villagers was exploited to create a pool of cheap labor available to Israel at substandard wages for jobs no Israeli would touch. The water resources of the West Bank were tapped not only for use by Israeli colonists but also for diversion to Israel proper. Even the planting of trees and the growing of vegetable patches by Palestinians were made subject to official Israeli permission.

Israeli policy centered on two complementary processes: the expropriation of land from or its closure to Palestinians; and the construction of Jewish colonies ("settlements") and towns on the land thus alienated, or its requisitioning for direct Israeli state use. Every nook and cranny of the legislation of the former regimes in Palestine (Jordanian, British, Ottoman, and pre-Ottoman) was searched for subterfuges by which to "legalize," rationalize, and gloss over the seizure of land whether from owners private or public, resident or absentee (in the diaspora); or from tenants, refugees, sharecroppers, shepherds, or Bedouins. Where no subterfuges could be devised, Palestinian soil was declared by fiat the "national patrimony" of the Jewish people. By 1984 nearly 50 percent of the West Bank and 30 percent of the Gaza Strip had been seized as "absentee property," or "registered state [i.e., Jordanian government] land," or land requisitioned for "military purposes" or closed for "training purposes," or land expropriated for "public purposes." In all instances land so seized was reserved for the exclusive use of the Israeli government or Jewish citizens of Israel.

The implantation of Jewish colonies and towns accompanied the process of land alienation. At first these colonies masqueraded as military or paramilitary outposts in uninhabited areas set up for "security" reasons or even as archaeological excavation camps. But emboldened principally by the acquiescence of the United States and its funding of the colonization process, successive Israeli governments proceeded to establish colonies and towns in the midst of thickly inhabited Palestinian areas in the name of the biblical right of return to *all* parts of Eretz Israel. By 1983 Jewish colonists were living in about 140 colonies and towns all over the Palestinian Occupied Territories. To be sure, a tiny proportion of the confiscated land (30,000 out of 2.15 million dunams*) had been owned by Jews in these territories before 1948; however, the restoration of property to its pre-1948 owners was exclusively restricted to Jews and did not apply to Palestinian-owned property in West Jerusalem and Israel proper.

The Palestinians and their PLO leadership in the diaspora saw with horror their compatriots in East Jerusalem, the Gaza Strip, and the West Bank facing dispossession by slow strangulation — a fate even worse than that endured by their fathers and mothers in the period culminating in 1948.

The PLO answered the historic delegitimization of Palestinians by Zionism with counterdelegitimization, and Israel terror with Palestinian terror. The more active the PLO the more steadfast the Palestinians were under occupation, and the more steadfast the Palestinians under occupation the more resolved the Israelis were to extirpate the roots of autonomous Palestinian decision-making, i.e., the civilian and military institutions of the PLO. Hence the Israeli devastation of the Jordan Valley (across which the PLO operated from Jordan) in the period from 1968 to 1970. Hence also the Israeli devastation of southern Lebanon and the suburbs of Beirut (the PLO's base of operations after 1971), culminating in the siege and bombardmenmt of the Lebanese capital and the massacre at Sabra and Shatila in 1982.

The distinctive lot of the Palestinians now (whether in the suburbs of Beirut, the Old City of Jerusalem, or elsewhere) is that their suffering, be it physical or mental, has little chance of fading into a distant memory: The wounds of yesterday fester alongside those of today.

A victim's obsession with the past is often the concomitant of a vengeful disposition, and protagonists have habitually compiled "historical records" of their conflicts as a prelude to each other's delegitimization. But a retrospective glance can also serve a constructive purpose. That is the intent of this book, which it is hoped will shed some light on the Palestinians as a people in Pal-

*One dunam equals one thousand square meters.

estine before their diaspora, and on the genesis and evolution of the Palestine problem during its formative phase. By so doing may it also foster an understanding of the Palestinian situation today and the minimal prerequisites for an honorable settlement, from the Palestinian perspective, against the background of the actual historical record.

Before Their Diaspora is limited in its chronological and topical scope; its core is the photographs and their captions. It deals neither with the Zionist venture per se nor with the Arab-Israeli conflict in general. The beginning of the period covered by the photographs (1876) was chosen for two reasons: The earliest photographs that could be found on the Palestinians go back to this time, and the earliest stirrings of Zionism in Eastern Europe happened to occur more or less simultaneously. The final date, 15 May 1948, marks the formal end of the British Mandate, the end of the "civil war" phase of the first Arab-Israeli war, the forcible establishment of the state of Israel, and the resultant beginning of the Palestinian diaspora. With few exceptions, no attempt was made to include photographs of related contemporaneous events occurring outside Palestine. Some of these events, however, are referred to in the introductions and chronologies. The historical introduction to Part I reaches back into antiquity.

The book is structured chronologically. Its five main parts deal, respectively, with the last days of Ottoman rule (1876–1918), the period from the British occupation to the Great Palestine Rebellion (1918–35), the Great Rebellion (1936–39), the period from the London Conference to the UN partition recommendation (1939–47), and the six months of civil war (November 1947–May 1948).

The photographs in Part I are somewhat loosely organized around aspects of political, social, cultural, and religious life, concluding with a "portrait gallery." Those in Parts II and IV are more rigidly organized into subsections along the same lines. The photographs in Parts III and V focus almost exclusively on the momentous political and military developments that occurred during the periods they cover. The photographs in Part I cover the longest period — some forty years;

those in Part V, the shortest — only six months. Every attempt was made to determine the exact date of each photograph, or failing that, to establish as accurate an approximation as possible, but within some subsections a strict chronological sequence is not always followed.

Most of the 474 photographs that appear here were selected from a total of about 10,000 photographs in the archives of the Institute for Palestine Studies, Beirut, now transferred to Geneva, Switzerland. The most precious collections in the IPS archives are those of the late Wasif Jawhariyyah and the late Khalil Raad, to which many photographs donated by or acquired from individual Palestinians and Arabs have been added. In preparing this volume, however, selections were also made from the photographic archives of several other institutions in Britain and the United States, which are mentioned below.

It was not an easy task to collect and identify photographs from individual Palestinians resident in so many countries. The deteriorating situation in Lebanon, where work on this book began, made the task all the harder. Numerous other relevant photographs to which access could not be obtained must, of course, exist in various institutions and private homes all over the world. A continued search for these photographs would no doubt have further enriched the selection published here, but for practical reasons it was necessary to end the search at some point.

The photographs in this book were chosen on the basis of their relevance to its purpose and subject matter. Content took precedence over aesthetic criteria, so that occasionally the content of even a poorly produced photograph justified its inclusion. The selection of photographs was also partly determined by the requirements of structure and balance within the various sections and subsections. In the last analysis, though, the photographs that appear here could only reflect the range of the total number from which they were chosen. While every effort was made to cover as many aspects of Palestinian life as possible, gaps inevitably remain and are readily noticeable.

Each photograph has two numbers: a sequence number and the catalogue number assigned to it either in the IPS archives or in the external col-

lection from which it was selected. In the commentaries, photographs are identified by sequence number only. The list of photographic credits on pp. 349–51 identifies the photographs by catalogue number also. Almost all the photographic reproductions for this book were made from copy prints, because the original photographs were not available.

On the perennial question of transliterating Arabic words into English, I have not followed any rigorous system. Thus I have dispensed with initial and terminal ains and hamzas, retaining only medial ones, e.g., Ka'bah (ain) and Samu'il (hamza). I have generally been guided by common usage and, in certain cases, by how individuals wished their names to appear in English.

Finally, a note on the term "Palestinian." Because of its increasingly exclusive use since 1948 to denote Palestinian *Arab*, it has been used throughout the book in this sense.

Many institutes and individuals have contributed to the preparation of this volume. Special thanks are due to the Imperial War Museum in London; the Matson Photo Service at the Episcopal Home in Alhambra, California; and the PLO Information Center in Beirut for permission to use photographs from their archives.

Dr. Fathi Qaddoura took a particular interest in this project on behalf of one of its two principal patrons, the Arab Bank Ltd., Amman. Prof. John Munro ably edited the first version of the captions. Ms. Juliana Peck and Rev. Daniel Harrington, S.J., read drafts of the introductions and preface, while Mr. Muhammad Ali Khalidi rechecked the commentaries, chronologies, and introductions for factual congruence; all three made valuable suggestions. Mr. and Mrs. Sa'id Abu Hamdeh were unstinting in their help with the development and production of the photographs. Ms. Martha Dukas very fortunately introduced me to Mr. Richard Zonghi, the designer.

Many of the photographs in this book were selected from the collection of the late Wasif Jawhariyyah of Jerusalem, a noted Palestinian connoisseur and arbiter of taste. Mr. Jawhariyyah deposited his entire priceless collection at the Institute for Palestine Studies, and I am particularly pleased and honored to have the opportunity of introducing at least a portion of his legacy to the general public. Extensive use has also been made of the unique collection of the late Khalil Raad of Jerusalem, the leading professional Palestinian photographer of his time. I wish to express my deep gratitude and appreciation to the families of both these worthy gentlemen.

A number of other individuals have also helped either by identifying photographs or by donating them from their family albums. I am sincerely thankful to all of them: Mr. and Mrs. Abd al-Rahman Abd al-Hadi, Ms. Soraya Antonius, Mrs. Hanna Asfour, Mr. Anton Attallah, Mrs. Mu'in Bisisu, Mr. Abdurrahman A. Bushnaq, Mr. Kamel Deeb, Dr. Salma Jayyusi, Mr. Salim Katul, Mr. and Mrs. Khulusi Khairi, Dr. Rashid Khalidi, Ms. Dominique Roch, Mr. Fuad Saba, Mr. Yusuf Shadid, Ms. Hilda George Shibr, Mr. and Mrs. Adel Taji, Dr. Izzat Tannous, Mr. Ghaleb Suleiman Tuqan, Mrs. Suha Tuqan, Mrs. Milli Ziyadeh, and Dr. Nicola Ziyadeh.

WALID KHALIDI

Cambridge, Massachusetts
15 November 1984

LIST OF MAPS

JERUSALEM: ALLAH'S CHOICE

1

"The choice of Allah of all his lands is Jerusalem . . . the dew which descends upon Jerusalem is a remedy from every sickness, because it is from the gardens of Paradise."[1]

1 This vast compound some thirty-four acres in area, known as the Haram al-Sharif (Noble Sanctuary), is situated in the Old City of Jerusalem, one of the three holiest cities of Islam (the other two being Mecca and Medina). In the early days of Islam, Muslims turned in prayer toward Jerusalem and not, as later, toward Mecca. The octagonal structure is the Mosque of the Dome of the Rock, built by the caliph Abd al-Malik between A.D. 688 and 691. It is the earliest Muslim monument surviving. Behind it is the Mosque of al-Aqsa, built by Abd al-Malik's son al-Walid during his caliphate (A.D. 705–715). The prophet Muhammad was transported from Mecca to Jerusalem in mystical flight on a wondrous steed, al-Buraq; he tethered the steed to a wall (extreme right), the outside of which is the Jewish Wailing Wall. From the rock under the dome, the Prophet ascended to heaven. The smaller cupolas and buildings in and around the compound are variously shrines, colleges, monasteries (of mystical brotherhoods), public fountains, and tombs of Muslim saints and scholars.

JESUS: ALLAH'S WORD

2

"The Messiah, Jesus, son of Mary . . . His word which He conveyed unto Mary, and a spirit from Him . . ."[1]

2 The Star of Bethlehem, Church of the Nativity. Islam is deeply imbued with Judeo-Christian beliefs and traditions. The prophet Muhammad is seen by Muslims as the last and "seal" (*khatim*) of a long line of earlier prophets. His Hebrew precursors are held in great reverence by Islam, as are the virgin Mary and Jesus. Bethlehem is one of several Palestinian towns inhabited almost exclusively by Christian Arabs, who constitute about 10 percent of all Palestinians.

PART I

THE LAST DAYS OF OTTOMAN RULE

1876–1918

INTRODUCTION

PALESTINE was the name applied by Herodotus and other Greek and Latin writers to the Philistine coastland, and sometimes also to the territory between it and the Jordan Valley. Early in the Roman Empire the name Palaestina was given to the region around Jerusalem. The Byzantines in turn named the province west of the Jordan River, stretching from Mount Carmel in the north to Gaza in the south, Palaestina Prima.

ROME AND BYZANTIUM

In A.D. 70 the Roman emperor Titus suppressed a Jewish revolt in Palestine, razed Jerusalem to the ground, and destroyed its Temple. After a second Jewish revolt (A.D. 132–135) the emperor Hadrian built a new, pagan city on the ruins of Jerusalem, which he called Colonia Aelia Capitolina and forbade Jews to enter. After Hadrian's reign the number of Christians living in Jerusalem rose steadily until, with the conversion to Christianity of the emperor Constantine I (died 337) and the pilgrimage to Jerusalem in 320 of his mother, Queen Helena, the Christian character of Jerusalem and Palestine began to predominate over the pagan. Constantine himself built the Church of the Holy Sepulcher, and his successors, particularly Justinian (died 565), covered the country with churches and religious monuments. The Byzantines allowed the Jews to enter Jerusalem only one day a year to weep by a stone on the site of the Temple, but in deference to Jesus' prediction in Matt. 24:2, they kept the site desolate.

ISLAM AND THE UMAYYADS

Long before the rise of Islam in the seventh century, there had been continuous intermingling between the Christian peoples of Palestine and the Arab inhabitants (some of whom were also Christians) to the south and east. At first the prophet Muhammad and his followers turned in their prayers to Jerusalem, not Mecca. According to the Koran, Muhammad was miraculously transported in nocturnal flight from Mecca to Jerusalem, whence he ascended in seven stages to the presence of God. To this day Muhammad's spiritual journey is celebrated throughout the Muslim world on the twenty-seventh day of the seventh month by the Muslim calendar. Centuries after the event, the Muslim accounts of Muhammad's ascension became a source of inspiration to Dante in the writing of the *Divine Comedy*.[1]

The Arabs captured Jerusalem from the Byzantines in 637. To show his respect for the city, Omar (the second caliph after the death of the Prophet) accepted its surrender in person and treated its inhabitants with extraordinary clemency and moderation. In the words of Sir William Fitzgerald: "Never in the sorry story of conquest up to that day, and rarely since, were such noble and generous sentiments displayed by a conquerer as those extended to Jerusalem by Omar."[2] Omar was anxious to identify the places associated with Muhammad's ascension. The rock from which the ascension had taken place was located with difficulty, as it lay buried under a dunghill. After cleansing the rock, Omar led his entourage (which included many Companions, i.e., close associates, of the Prophet) in prayer beside it. The call to prayer was made for the first time since Muhammad's death by Bilal, his muezzin. One of the Companions who attended the ceremony, Ubadah, was appointed by Omar as first *qadi* ("judge") of Jerusalem and died in the city while holding that office. The Arabic name given to Jerusalem was al-Bait al-Muqaddas (the Holy House) in apposition to al-Bait al-Haram (the Sacred House), Mecca's designation. The Byzantine province of Palaestina Prima became the administrative and military province (*djund*) of Filastin — the Arabic name for Palestine since then.

Palestine was particularly honored by the Umayyad Arab dynasty (661–750), whose capital was Damascus. Mu'awiya (661–680), the founder of the dynasty, had himself proclaimed caliph in Jerusalem. One of his successors, the fifth Umayyad caliph, Abd al-Malik (685–705), built the magnificent Mosque of the Dome of the Rock over the rock from which Muhammad had ascended to heaven; Abd al-Malik's son Walid (705–715) built the adjacent Mosque of al-Aqsa. The Mosque of the Dome of the Rock, a dazzling synthesis of Byzantine, Persian, and Arab architecture, is the earliest surviving Muslim monument anywhere. The area of the two mosques became known as al-Haram al-Sharif (the Noble Sanctuary). The Umayyads' preference for Palestine and Jerusalem was in part politically motivated, because during the earlier decades of the dynasty Mecca and Medina were in the hands of rivals. But their attitude was also rooted in the Traditions (i.e., sayings) of the Prophet, some of the most famous of which equated Jerusalem with Mecca and Medina. It was to these Traditions that the Umayyads appealed when they urged Muslims to perform the pilgrimage at Jerusalem instead of in the two other holy cities. Thus even after Mecca and Medina came under Umayyad control in 692, the seventh Umayyad caliph, Suleiman (715–717), had himself invested with the caliphate in Jerusalem; he also built the city of Ramleh in Palestine, which he made his residence and adorned with a magnificent mosque and palace. Long after the Umayyads, the magnetic pull of Jerusalem was noted by the Persian traveler Nasir-i-Khusrau, who on visiting the city in 1047, wrote: "The people of these parts, if they are unable to make the pilgrimage to Mecca, will go at the appointed season to Jerusalem."[3]

THE ABBASIDS

The Abbasid dynasty (750–1225), with its seat in Baghdad, succeeded the Umayyads. It reached the zenith of its power and influence within a century of its foundation. Thereafter many provinces of the empire fell under local Muslim rulers holding only nominal allegiance to the Abbasid caliph, whose role now resembled that of the Holy Roman emperor after the decline of his power. For the greater part of the period from the end of the ninth century until the Crusades, Palestine was governed by Muslim rulers based in Cairo.

At the height of their power, two Abbasid caliphs made the pilgrimage to Jerusalem. Al-Mansur, the second Abbasid caliph (754–775), visited Jerusalem twice and ordered the repair of damage to the city caused by an earthquake. Al-Mahdi, the third Abbasid caliph (775–785), visited Jerusalem especially to pray at the al-Aqsa Mosque. The seventh Abbasid caliph, al-Ma'mun (813–833), ordered major restorations to be carried out in the Mosque of the Dome of the Rock under the supervision of his brother and successor, al-Mu'tasim (833–842), who was then his viceroy in Syria. So anxious were the Abbasids to be associated with Jerusalem that they ineptly substituted in inscriptions on the dome the name of al-Ma'mun for the Umayyad Abd al-Malik as the builder of the mosque.

Descriptions of Palestine in the centuries preceding the Crusades abound in the writings of Muslim and Arab geographers. Ya'kubi from Khorasan noted in 891–892 that Palestine had "a numerous population of Arabs . . . and a certain proportion of non-Muslims, Christians, Jews and Samaritans."[4] Ibn-al-Fakih from Hamadhan, who wrote in 903, related the Traditions about Jerusalem and gave detailed descriptions of its mosques. Ibn-Abd Rabih (died 940) from Cordova described the Dome of the Rock as well as other Muslim sanctuaries in Jerusalem, as did Istakhri (fl. 950) from Persepolis, closely followed by ibn-Hawkal (died 977). Overshadowing all of these accounts is the work of Muqqadasi (died 986), a native of Jerusalem. He enumerated the principal products of Palestine, "among which agricultural produce was particularly copious and prized: fruit of every kind (olives, figs, grapes, quinces, plums, apples, dates, walnuts, almonds, jujubes and bananas), some of which were exported, and crops for processing (sugarcane, indigo and sumac). But the mineral resources were equally important: chalk earth . . . marble from Bayt Djibrin, and sulphur mined in the Ghawr [Jordan Valley] not to mention the salt and bitumen of the Dead Sea. Stone, which was common in the country, was the most generally used building material for towns of any importance."[5]

In the wake of the caliphs from Omar onward, pious men and women in their thousands made the pilgrimage to Jerusalem. Jerusalem exerted a powerful attraction on the adherents of the mystical Sufi movement from its beginnings in the eighth century. For example, Rabi'a al-Adawiyah (ca. 717–801), a woman mystic accorded first place in the list of Muslim saints, who preached a life of "penitence, patience, gratitude, holy fear, voluntary poverty and utter dependence (*tawakkul*) upon God,"[6] chose to leave her native Basra in Iraq in order to live, meditate, and die in Jerusalem. In addition to ordinary pilgrims and mystics, Jerusalem attracted a steady flow of scholars: experts in Koranic exegesis and in the Traditions, theologians and grammarians who came to write and lecture in the city's grand mosques and the dozens of colleges affiliated with them.

The greatest of these scholars was al-Ghazzali (1058–1111), the leading theologian of Islam and one of its most original thinkers. Al-Ghazzali left his post as lecturer at the prestigious Nizamiyah Academy in Baghdad in 1095 to take up residence in Jerusalem, where he began work on his magnum opus, *The Revivification of the Sciences of Religion*, a magisterial reconciliation of rationalism, mysticism, and legal orthodoxy which, in addition to revitalizing Islamic theology, left its mark through partial Latin translations on Jewish and Christian scholasticism. Also in Jerusalem, at the insistence of his students there, al-Ghazzali completed a concise exposition of the Muslim creed, calling it *The Jerusalem Tract*.

Omar had allowed Christians the undisturbed use of their churches in Jerusalem. His successors strictly maintained this policy except for some serious outbreaks of anti-Christian fanaticism in Jerusalem in 966 (in which Jews took part with Muslims), and again in 1009. Otherwise Christian pilgrimage to the holy places continued uninterrupted. The Abbasid caliph Harun al-Rashid (786–809), of legendary fame, acceded to Charlemagne's request that hostels for Christian pilgrims be established in Palestine and nuns be permitted to serve in Jerusalem.

Jews had been debarred from living in Jerusalem first by the Romans under Hadrian and then by the Christian Byzantines. In their negotiations for the surrender of the city to Omar, the Christian inhabitants probably demanded that the ban on the residence of Jews be included in the treaty of surrender. Nevertheless, Omar's successors deviated from the terms of the treaty with regard to the Jews, and gradually allowed Jews to take up residence in the city. The first mention of a synagogue in Jerusalem after Hadrian seems to be one made by the Persian traveler Nasir-i-Khusrau in 1047.[7]

THE CRUSADES AND COUNTER-CRUSADES

Arab and Muslim rule over Palestine was interrupted by the Crusader invasion and the establishment of the Latin kingdom of Jerusalem (1099–1187). The counter-Crusades, led by Saladin (died 1193) and his successors, persisted until 1291, when the last Frankish strongholds, Caesarea and Acre, were retaken. After their entry into Jerusalem, the Crusaders had tortured, burnt, and massacred thousands of defenseless Muslims (men, women, and children) as well as the small number of Jewish residents who had taken refuge in their synagogue. By contrast, Saladin's entry into Jerusalem in 1187, at the pinnacle of his military might, displayed the same reverence for the city and compassion for its Christian inhabitants that the caliph Omar had shown some five hundred years earlier. As Stanley Lane-Poole commented: "If the taking of Jerusalem were the only fact known about Saladin, it were enough to prove him the most chivalrous and great-hearted conqueror of his own, and perhaps of any, age."[8]

Saladin's first task after entering Jerusalem was to cleanse the Dome of the Rock and the al-Aqsa Mosque of defilement. For a whole week, noble and humble men alongside each other washed the walls and floors of the buildings and sprinkled them with rose water. The relatives and descendants of the Muslim inhabitants of Jerusalem (who had been made refugees by the Crusader conquest of the city) were given back their family properties; and where no owners could be found, the dwellings were assigned to well-known Arab clans. Saladin introduced the institution of the *madrasah* ("collegiate mosque") into Jerusalem and endowed one bearing his name (al-Sala-hiyyah). He also endowed a hospital and two hostels for scholars and mystics. The soldiers who had died in his campaign were buried outside the Gate of Mercy on the eastern side of the Haram al-Sharif (Noble Sanctuary) by his command. In 1193 Saladin's son al-Afdal built the Magharibah Mosque near the gate of the same name on the southwest side of the Haram; this was the site where Muhammad had tethered his wondrous mount before his ascension. Al-Afdal dedicated the land outside the gate as *waqf* ("religious endowment") for the mosque and for pilgrims and scholars from North Africa.

Saladin and his successors, the Ayyubids, allowed Christians to reside and practice their faith in Jerusalem; and the city was kept open to Christian pilgrims from Europe, although the fear persisted for centuries that the Franks might attempt to reconquer it. The number of Jews residing in Jerusalem under the Crusaders had declined to one, a dyer, noted by the Jewish traveler Rabbi Pethahiah of Regensburg (ca. 1177). But Saladin and his successors revived the Jewish presence in Jerusalem. Indeed, after the Crusades all the lands of Islam became a haven for Jews from Europe, inasmuch as the Crusades were equally anti-Semitic and anti-Muslim.

The Crusades and counter-Crusades inspired a resurgence of intense Muslim and Arab interest in Palestine, which took three forms: (1) A host of writers and poets celebrated the religious significance and value of Jerusalem in a new literary genre known as the Books of Virtues (Fada'il). The themes of these works were the special efficacy of prayers offered in the city and the advantages of pilgrimage to it or residence and death in it. But Jerusalem was not the only place singled out for veneration. Great emphasis was laid both on Muslim tombs and shrines in different parts of the country (e.g., the tomb of Hashim, grandfather of Muhammad, at Gaza) and on sites associated with the Hebrew prophets — tombs or reputed tombs and birthplaces or spots the prophets had visited or dwelt in. (2) Pilgrimages and visits to Palestine multiplied and became a popular regional phenomenon. (3) Competition arose among Muslim rulers and affluent individuals to build public institutions (schools, hostels, soup kitchens, clinics, baths, and fountains) as endowments for the mosques and other Muslim shrines in Palestine.

This resurgence of Muslim and Arab interest in Filastin/Palestine was no passing mood in mere reaction to the Crusader threat. During the seventeenth and eighteenth centuries, for example, it took yet another form. The pilgrimage to Jerusalem became a central tenet of many Sufi *tariqahs* ("brotherhoods"). The Mosque of the Dome of the Rock in Jerusalem (which housed the rock from which Muhammad ascended to heaven) became the site of special rituals and elevating experiences. There the mentors of the *tariqahs* would instruct their disciples in programs of rigorous fasting and contemplation. Special prayer sessions known as *dhikrs* ("recollections") were held at which the attributes of God and the Prophet were repeatedly recollected in such variations as to induce a state of religious ecstasy. These sessions were in preparation for the climactic experience of identification, at the very site of the Prophet's ascension, with the Prophet's own imagined spiritual state during his ascension. For to the Sufis, Muhammad's ascension symbolized the soul's escape from its corporeal moorings. Palestinian and other Arab adherents of Sufi *tariqahs* are still found today.

THE MAMELUKES

In 1260 power passed from the hands of Saladin's descendants, the Ayyubids, to those of the Mameluke sultans of Egypt. From that date until the Ottoman conquest of Egypt in 1517, Palestine remained part of the Mameluke realm. It was the Mamelukes who drove the last Crusaders out of Palestine and who in 1260, at the battle of Ayn Jalut near Nazareth, defeated the Mongol hordes under Hulagu, grandson of Genghis Khan, saving the country from certain destruction. Except during the period of the Crusades, the administrative unit of the *djund* of Filastin, established by the caliph Omar, had been maintained. The Mamelukes reorganized the country administratively by dividing it into six districts: those of Gaza, Lydda, Kakun (after a village north of Lydda), Jerusalem, Hebron, and Nablus. These territories west of the Jordan River continued to serve as a major crossroads linking Cairo with Damascus and Aleppo, traversed as much by merchants as by administrators, pilgrims, and couriers.

The Mamelukes granted Jerusalem special favors. Several of the sultans lightened its taxes or presented splendid copies of the Koran to its mosques, while most undertook repairs and additions (e.g., colonnades and minarets) to its sanctuaries. Sultan Baibars (1260–77) built a khan, or inn, for the relief of the poor, and Sultan al-Ashraf Ka'it Bay (1468–95) rebuilt on a grand scale a *madrasah* that still bears his name (al-Ashrafiyyah). Muslim geographers made frequent mention of Palestine and Jerusalem during this period, among them Yakut (1179–1229) from Asia Minor; Abul Fida (1273–1332), a descendant of Saladin's brother; and ibn-Battuta (1304–77) from Tangiers. They recounted the references to Jerusalem in the Koran and the Traditions, and described its mosques, sanctuaries, schools, bazaars, inns, and pious foundations. Most important for Jerusalem as well as Hebron under the Mamelukes is the work written in 1495 by the *qadi* of Jerusalem Mujir al-Din, who also listed the names of famous Muslim scholars, soldiers, rulers, and mystics buried in the city, in addition to the many Jerusalemites who attained high office in the service of the Mamelukes.

THE OTTOMANS

From 1516 until the end of World War I, the whole region of western Asia was part of the Ottoman Empire. The majestic superstructure of the walls encircling the Old City of Jerusalem, built by the Ottoman sultan Suleiman the Magnificent (1520–66), attests to Jerusalem's standing in Ottoman eyes. Equally revealing is the endowment made in 1552 by Khasseki Sultan (known in Europe as Roxelana), the favorite and queen of Suleiman. Seeking "the pleasure of Allah," she built a complex in Jerusalem "for the poor and the needy, the weak and the distressed" that included a monastery "with fifty-five doors" and an inn together with a public kitchen, bakery, stables, and storerooms. The endowment deed specified the range of employees required to run this institution — stewards, clerks, master cooks (and ap-

prentices), food inspectors, dishwashers, millers, handymen, and garbage collectors. It described in detail the menus to be served, the ingredients to be used, and the quantities to be cooked. For the maintenance of the establishment, it set aside the revenues from twenty-three Palestinian villages as well as those from a village in northern Lebanon, and shops and soap factories in Tripoli.[9] Khasseki Sultan's public kitchen and bakery were still functioning under the British Mandate.

The Ottomans scrupulously continued the Muslim tradition of tolerance toward Christian religious interests in Palestine. The Greek Orthodox Patriarchate in Jerusalem was acknowledged in the sixteenth century as the custodian of the Christian holy places, and from about the same time France became the guardian of the Latin clergy. Like earlier Muslim powers, the Ottoman Empire opened its gates to hundreds of thousands of Jewish refugees fleeing persecution in Spain and other parts of Christendom. But the vast majority, as in the earlier centuries after the Crusades, did not choose to live in Palestine. Thus the number of Jews in Jerusalem in the first century after the Ottoman conquest dropped from 1,330 in 1525 to 980 in 1587.[10] Even by the middle of the nineteenth century, only a few Jews had availed themselves of the opportunity to settle in the Holy Land. Those who did so lived in the four cities of special significance to Judaism: Jerusalem, Hebron, Safed, and Tiberias. The Ottomans presided over a set of regulations and understandings, known as the "status quo," that governed privileges and access rights of Jews and Christians at their respective religious sites and monuments. These regulations and understandings were based on customary practice as it had accumulated over the years. They included rights acknowledged by earlier Muslim rulers and the decisions of Muslim courts in support of these rights, as well as Christian and Jewish commitment to adhere to customary practice.

The activities of European merchants in the coastal towns of Palestine were unimpeded by the Ottomans. The agricultural and industrial products of the interior found their way to Europe via the ports of Gaza, Acre, and Jaffa. As before, the overland trade routes between Syria and Egypt passed through Palestine, while the pilgrimage routes to Mecca (whether from Cairo, Damascus, or beyond) converged at the Palestinian port of Aqaba. By the mid-nineteenth century, many European powers had consulates in the country, and during the second half of the century Christian missions — Catholic, Protestant, and Greek Orthodox — proliferated along with their schools, hospitals, printing presses, and hostels. In 1892 a French company completed the building of a railroad connecting Jaffa and Jerusalem. Of all the Arab provinces in the Ottoman Empire, with the exception of the Maronite sections of Mount Lebanon, Palestine was the most exposed and accessible to Christian European influences.

This exposure also had its disadvantages, particularly with the gradual decline of Ottoman political and military power. The industrial revolution and the European economic penetration of the region dealt a severe blow to local crafts and industries, while increasing European political leverage against Constantinople. One much-abused avenue for such leverage was afforded by the so-called Capitulations — a system of extraterritorial privileges granted to nationals of European powers who resided in the Ottoman Empire. The early Zionist immigrants and settlers were to make full use of the Capitulations.

In 1887–88, the area that later became Mandatory Palestine was divided into three administrative units: the district (*sanjak*) of Jerusalem, comprising the southern half of the country; and the two northern districts of Nablus and Acre. The two northern districts were administratively attached to the province (*vilayet*) of Beirut, but because of its importance to the Ottomans, the district of Jerusalem was governed directly by Constantinople. The area across the Jordan River (Trans-Jordan or Jordan) was administratively separate from the Palestinian districts and formed part of the province of Syria, with Damascus as its capital. At this time the population of the three Palestinian districts was ca. 600,000, about 10 percent of whom were Christians and the rest mostly Sunnite Muslims. The Jews numbered about 25,000; the majority were deeply religious, devoting themselves to prayer and contemplation and deliberately eschewing employment or agricultural activity. Until the advent of Zionism, relations between Palestinians and Jews were stable and peaceful, mellowed by more than a millennium of coexistence and often shared adversity.

Contributing to the climate of tolerance was the reverence held by Islam for the Hebrew prophets, enhanced in the case of Palestine by the tradition of pilgrimage to biblical sites. Palestinian Muslims, more than any other Muslims, were particularly imbued with such reverence if only because they lived in continuous proximity to the sites associated with these prophets. The inscription over Jaffa Gate (the main western gate into the Old City of Jerusalem) reads: "There is no God but Allah, and Abraham is his friend." Mosques and Muslim shrines honoring Hebrew prophets and bearing their names in Arabic were regular features of the Palestinian landscape. Perhaps unique among Muslims was the Palestinian practice of celebrating religious festivals in honor of Hebrew prophets. No less distinctive was the widespread use by Palestinians of Hebrew first names. The same tolerance is evident in the attitudes of Palestinian Muslims toward their Christian compatriots, relations with whom have been remarkably free of tension (unlike the situation in some neighboring Arab countries). It is no coincidence that the various Christian sects in Jerusalem have traditionally entrusted the keys of the Holy Sepulcher to a Palestinian Muslim family.

Although proud of their Arab heritage and ancestry, the Palestinians considered themselves to be descended not only from the Arab conquerors of the seventh century but also from indigenous peoples who had lived in the country since time immemorial, including the ancient Hebrews and the Canaanites before them. Acutely aware of the distinctiveness of Palestinian history, the Palestinians saw themselves as the heirs of its rich associations. Politically their loyalty was to Constantinople, partly because the Ottoman sultan was also caliph and head of the Muslim community (*ummah*) and partly because they felt like citizens rather than subjects of the empire. Their feeling of citizenship derived from the fact that the Ottoman Turks had never colonized the Arab provinces in the sense of settling in them; thus among the Arabs Ottomanism had acquired the connotation of partnership between the peoples of the empire rather than that of domination by

one ethnic group over another. Nevertheless, relations between the different ethnic groups
within the empire became increasingly strained
during the period from the turn of the century to
World War I, largely under the influence of growing European nationalism. Both Arabs and Turks
were affected by this climate, which strength-
ened the appeal of the specific ethnic and political identity of each. A powerful secondary
influence in the same direction was the Arab intellectual and literary renaissance that crystallized toward the end of the nineteenth century
and radiated its influence from Cairo, Damascus,
and Beirut.

The promulgation of the new Ottoman Constitution in 1876 (short-lived as it was) enabled the
first elections to be held to the Ottoman Parliament, in which many delegates from the Arab
provinces, including Palestinians from Jerusalem,
took their seats. (It is ironic that Palestinians
were sitting in the Parliament in Constantinople
twenty years before the Zionists held their first
congress in Basel in 1897.) Arabs, including Palestinians, were appointed to high office not only
in the civil service, the diplomatic corps, the judiciary, and the army, but also as ministers in
the Ottoman cabinet. The "Young Turks" Revolution in 1908, which brought reformists to
power, further raised Arab and Palestinian expec-
tations, stimulating political debate and intellectual activity best exemplified in Palestine by the
appearance of new journals and newspapers. Delegates from Jerusalem, Jaffa, Nablus, Acre, and
Gaza were elected to the Ottoman Parliament in
1908 and 1912. But Ottoman reforms could not
keep abreast of deteriorating Turkish-Arab relations. Many Arabs wanted a greater share in government. Some advocated decentralization;
others spoke of Arab unity, revolt, and independence.

ZIONISM AND WORLD WAR I

Meanwhile, during the 1880s an important development in Eastern Europe began to cast its
lengthening shadow on the future of the Palestinians. The phenomena of European nationalism
and colonialism had inspired a national political
movement known as Zionism among a growing

number of East European Jewish intellectuals.
The Zionists yearned to escape from Jewish minority status and the twin threats of assimilation
and persecution. They saw the acquisition of territory where a Jewish sovereign state could be established as the means of national fulfillment and
salvation. The ancient Jewish association with
and religious attachment to Palestine were regarded as justifying its choice as the site for such
a state, though some early Zionists were willing
to consider alternative sites.

The Zionist decision, late in the nineteenth
century, to colonize Palestine with a view to
turning it into a Jewish state irrespective of the
existence and wishes of its indigenous population ushered in the turbulent modern phase of
Palestinian history, whose consequences are with
us today. The course set by the Zionists was
bound to lead to conflict and tragedy, an outcome foreseen by some Zionist leaders themselves. For Palestine, as we have seen, was *not* an
empty land. Its inhabitants lived in a score of cities and towns, and some eight hundred villages
and hamlets, built of stone. While the bulk of the
population gained their living from agriculture,
the townspeople engaged in commerce and the
traditional crafts; some were in the civil service,
others in the professions. Many of the urban rich
were landlords, but members of the older families were also in the upper echelons of the civil
service, the judiciary, and the professions. The
Palestinians, both Christian and Muslim, formed
a proud and vibrant community that had already
crossed the threshold of an intellectual and national renaissance. They shared and reflected the
cultural and political values of the neighboring
Arab metropolitan centers. For centuries they had
had trade links with Europe and contact with Europeans who came as Christian pilgrims to the
Holy Land. For decades they had been exposed to
modernizing influences as a result of the educational and medical work of European and American Christian missions. Service in the European
and Asian provinces of the Ottoman Empire had
widened their horizons.

The Palestinians were as deeply entrenched in
their country on the eve of the Zionist venture
as any citizenry or peasantry anywhere. The contemporaneous photographic collection of Félix

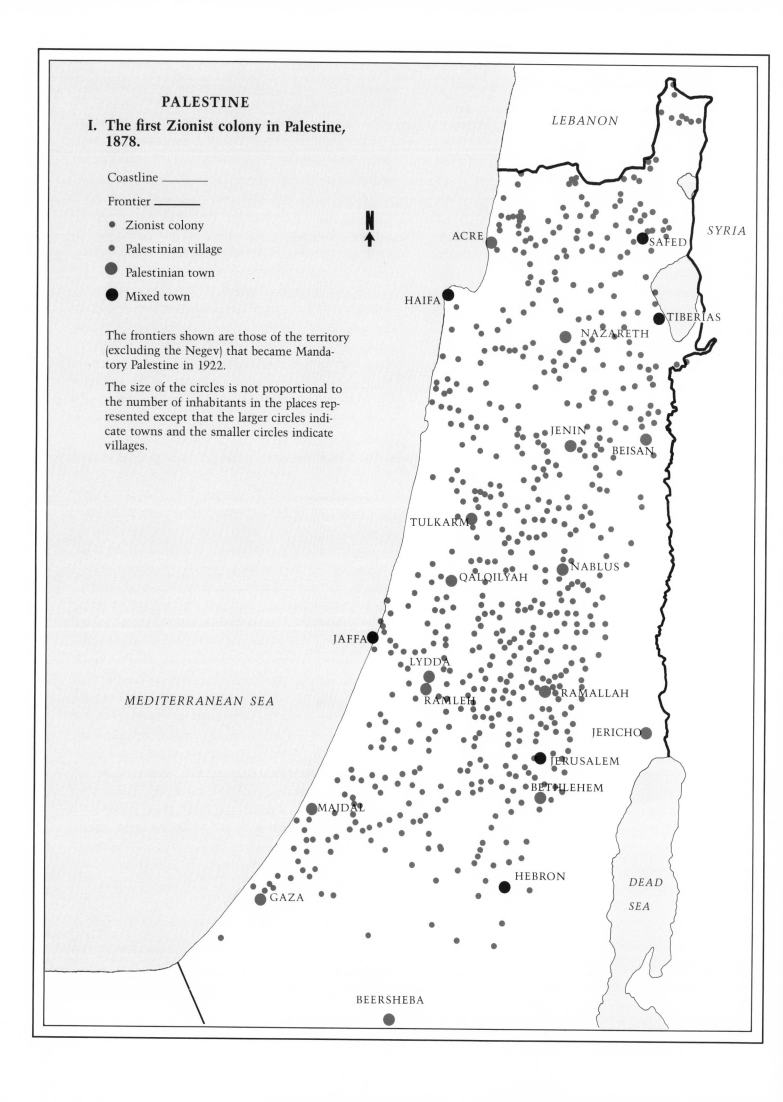

PALESTINE

I. The first Zionist colony in Palestine, 1878.

Coastline ———

Frontier ———

• Zionist colony

• Palestinian village

● Palestinian town

● Mixed town

The frontiers shown are those of the territory (excluding the Negev) that became Mandatory Palestine in 1922.

The size of the circles is not proportional to the number of inhabitants in the places represented except that the larger circles indicate towns and the smaller circles indicate villages.

N

LEBANON

SYRIA

ACRE

HAIFA

SAFED

TIBERIAS

NAZARETH

JENIN

BEISAN

TULKARM

NABLUS

QALQILYAH

MEDITERRANEAN SEA

JAFFA

LYDDA

RAMLEH

RAMALLAH

JERICHO

JERUSALEM

BETHLEHEM

MAJDAL

HEBRON

DEAD SEA

GAZA

BEERSHEBA

Bonfils (1831–85) and his son Adrien (1860–1929) is visual testimony to this fact. No less telling is the evidence of the many European artists and painters who visited Palestine before the advent of Zionism, e.g., William Henry Bartlett (1809–54), David Roberts (1796–1864), Edward Lear (1812–88), and William Holman Hunt (1827–1910). After all, the Palestinians' main grievance against Constantinople was that they wanted greater recognition of their rights and more responsibility in government; they were altogether unlikely to acquiesce in the Zionist political program, which challenged their very title to their land.

The first Zionist colony in Palestine was founded in 1878, and the first wave of Zionist immigrants arrived in 1882. In the same year a French Jewish millionaire, Baron Edmond de Rothschild, began his support of Jewish colonization in Palestine. In 1896 a German Jewish millionaire, Baron Maurice de Hirsch, established a branch of his Jewish Colonization Association in Palestine, while Theodor Herzl, a Hungarian Jew, published *Der Judenstaat* — a treatise that integrated prevailing Zionist ideas and outlined a program of implementation. The following year in Basel, Switzerland, Herzl convened the First Zionist Congress, which created the World Zionist Organization, the institutional framework for subsequent Zionist diplomacy and operations. In 1901 the Keren Kayemeth (Jewish National Fund) was established in London to acquire land in Palestine that would remain inalienably Jewish and on which only Jewish labor would be employed. Between the 1880s and 1914 some thirty Zionist colonies were founded, and by 1914 the total Jewish population in Palestine had reached about eighty thousand, although the majority retained their European nationalities.

The initial phases of Zionist activity in Palestine took place in spite of the mounting alarm and opposition of the Palestinians. The Ottoman authorities repeatedly tried to legislate controls on Zionist mass immigration and land acquisition only to be frustrated by the pressure of European powers, the corruption of their own local officials, the greed of individual landowners, and Zionist ingenuity in exploiting the Capitulations system. The earliest tensions between Palestinians and Jews developed as a result of the colonizing program and declared political purposes of European Zionist immigrants. Vast estates were purchased by the central Zionist institutions from feudal absentee landlords in Beirut, over the heads of Palestinian tenants and sharecroppers.

World War I brought Britain and those Arabs who were dissatisfied with Ottoman rule into an alliance with each other. Sharif Hussein of Mecca hoped, by siding with Britain and the Western Allies against Constantinople, to win unity and independence for the Arabs at the end of the war. In July 1915 Hussein undertook a correspondence in good faith with Sir Henry McMahon, the British high commissioner of Egypt. Concluded in 1916, the Hussein-McMahon correspondence was interpreted by the Arabs to mean that, in the postwar settlement, the British would recognize the independence of a united Arab state comprising the Arab provinces of the Ottoman Empire, including Palestine. By May 1916, however, Britain, France, and Russia had reached a secret agreement according to which the bulk of Palestine was to be internationalized. More significant for future developments was a secret letter addressed in November 1917 by Arthur James Balfour, British secretary of state for foreign affairs, to Baron Lionel Walter de Rothschild, a British Zionist, promising British support for the establishment in Palestine of a national home for the Jewish people. This document marked the historic watershed in the fortunes of Zionism. Jerusalem was captured by British and Dominion forces under the command of General Sir Edmund Allenby in December 1917. The rest of the country was occupied by October 1918. The road to the realization of Zionism lay wide open.

CHRONOLOGY

1876 Ottoman Constitution promulgated.

1876–1877 First Ottoman Parliament convenes in Constantinople; first Palestinian deputies from Jerusalem elected to this Parliament.

1878 Petah Tikva, first Zionist colony, established in Palestine.

1881 November: Ottoman government announces permission for foreign (non-Ottoman) Jews to settle throughout Ottoman Empire excluding Palestine.

1882 Baron Edmond de Rothschild of Paris begins financial backing of Jewish colonization in Palestine.

First wave of Zionist mass immigration to Palestine begins.

Jewish population of Palestine numbers 24,000.

July: Ottoman government adopts policy allowing Jewish pilgrims and businessmen to visit Palestine but not to settle there.

December: Ottoman government informs Jewish leadership in Constantinople that it views Zionist colonization in Palestine as political problem.

1884 March: Ottoman government decides to close Palestine to foreign (non-Ottoman) Jewish businessmen but not to Jewish pilgrims.

1888 May: European powers pressure Ottoman government to allow foreign (non-Ottoman) Jews to settle in Palestine provided they do so singly and not en masse.

1891 German Jewish millionaire Baron Maurice de Hirsch founds Jewish Colonization Association (JCA).

Ottoman Sultan Abd-al Hamid II expresses fears that granting Ottoman nationality to Jewish immigrants in Palestine "may result in the creation of a Jewish Government in Jerusalem."

1892 November: Ottoman government forbids sale of state land to foreign (non-Ottoman) Jews in Palestine.

1893 April: European powers pressure Ottoman government to permit Jews legally resident in Palestine to buy land provided they establish no colonies on it.

1896 JCA begins operations in Palestine.

Publication of *Der Judenstaat*, by Hungarian Zionist leader Theodor Herzl, advocating creation of Jewish state in Argentina or Palestine.

Abd-al Hamid II rejects Herzl's proposal that Palestine be granted to the Jews: "I cannot give away any part of it [the Empire]. . . . I will not agree to vivisection."

1897 Commission headed by Muhammad Tahir al-Husseini, mufti (highest Muslim religious dignitary) of Jerusalem, appointed to scrutinize Zionist land-acquisition methods.

August: First Zionist Congress, convening in Basel, Switzerland, issues Basel Program on colonization of Palestine and establishment of World Zionist Organization (WZO).

In response to First Zionist Congress, Abd-al Hamid II initiates policy of sending members of his own palace staff to govern province of Jerusalem.

1898 Arabic press reacts to First Zionist Congress. Cairo journal *al-Manar* warns that Zionism aims to take possession of Palestine.

Kaiser Wilhelm II of Germany visits Jerusalem.

1899 October: Albert Antebi, JCA representative in Jerusalem, observes that program of First Zionist Congress has adversely affected relations between Palestinians and Jewish immigrants.

March 19: Herzl sends letter to Palestinian mayor of Jerusalem hinting that, if Zionists not welcome in Palestine, they will go elsewhere.

1900 JCA takes responsibility for colonies supported by Baron de Rothschild.

June: Ottoman government sends commission of inquiry to Palestine to study implications of Zionist mass immigration and land acquisition.

1901 Pressured by European powers, Ottoman government allows foreign (non-Ottoman) Jews to buy land in northern Palestine.

Keren Kayemeth (Jewish National Fund) founded as land-acquisition organ of WZO; land acquired by JNF in Palestine to be inalienably Jewish, and exclusively Jewish labor to be employed on it.

January: Ottoman restrictions on Zionist immigration to and land acquisition in Jerusalem district take effect.

May: Administrative Council of Jerusalem strongly objects to JCA's attempts at acquiring land in Jerusalem district.

July: Palestinian peasants in region of Tiberias express alarm at extent of Zionist land acquisition.

1902 January: *Al-Manar* warns that Zionism seeks national sovereignty in Palestine.

February: JCA representative Antebi observes that "the ill will of the local population coincides with the creation of Zionism."

1903 Second wave of Zionist mass immigration to Palestine begins.

December: Anglo-Palestine Company (APC), subsidiary of JCA, established in Palestine to finance Zionist colonization.

1904 July: Death of Theodor Herzl.

August–September: Tensions develop between Zionist colonists and Palestinian farmers in region of Tiberias.

1905 Publication of *Le Reveil de la Nation Arabe*, by Negib Azoury, warning of Zionist political aims in Palestine.

1907 First kibbutz, based on exclusively Jewish labor, established.

August: Report issued by Ottoman governor of Jerusalem on Zionist evasion of Ottoman immigration and land-transfer regulations.

1908 Palestinian deputies from Jerusalem, Jaffa, Nablus, and Acre elected to Ottoman Parliament of 1908 in Constantinople.

Palestinian journal *al-Karmil* founded in Haifa with purpose of opposing Zionist colonization.

March 16: Clash between Zionist immigrants and Palestinians in Jaffa results in one Palestinian dead and 13 Jews wounded.

July 24: Beginning of "Young Turks" Revolution in Constantinople.

1909 Tel Aviv founded north of Jaffa.

February–April: Renewed tensions and clashes between Zionist colonists and Palestinian farmers near Nazareth.

June: Zionist issue raised for first time in Ottoman Parliament by Palestinian deputy from Jaffa.

July: Five members of Ottoman Parliament, including Palestinian deputy from Jerusalem, meet with British Zionist leader Sir Francis Montefiore in London to voice their concern about political objectives of Zionism.

1910 Arabic newspapers in Beirut, Damascus, and Haifa express opposition to Zionist land acquisition in Palestine.

June: Deputies in Ottoman Parliament from Arab provinces request assurances from Ottoman minister of interior against Zionist land-acquisition policies in Palestine.

1911 Palestinian journalist Najib Nassar publishes first book in Arabic on Zionism, entitled *Zionism: Its History, Objective and Importance*.

January–February: European powers pressure Ottoman government to allow Zionist land acquisition in Palestine.

January: Palestinian newspaper *Filastin* begins to appear; addressing its readers as "Palestinians," it warns them about consequences of Zionist colonization.

March–April: Arab deputies from Jerusalem, Beirut, and Damascus lobby in Ottoman Parliament for legislation against Zionist mass immigration to Palestine.

April: In telegram to Constantinople, 150 Palestinians from Jaffa demand measures against Zionist mass immigration and land acquisition.

May 16: Two Jerusalem deputies open first full-scale debate in Ottoman Parliament on Zionism, charging that Zionist aim is to create Jewish state in Palestine.

1912 Palestinian deputies from Jerusalem, Gaza, Nablus, and Acre elected to Ottoman Parliament of 1912.

January: European powers renew pressure on Ottoman government to facilitate Zionist land acquisition in Palestine.

1913 January: Palestinian contributor to *Filastin* writes: "The Zionists will gain mastery over our country village by village, town by town."

1914 August 1: Outbreak of World War I.

1915 July 14: Correspondence between Sharif Hussein of Mecca and Sir Henry McMahon, British high commissioner in Egypt, begins.

August: Jemal Pasha, Ottoman military governor, hangs 11 Arab nationalists in Beirut.

1916 January 30: Hussein-McMahon correspondence concludes; Arabs understand it as ensuring postwar independence and unity of Arab provinces of Ottoman Empire, including Palestine.

May: Jemal Pasha hangs 21 Arab leaders and intellectuals, including two Palestinians, in Beirut and Damascus.

May 16: Signing of secret Sykes-Picot Agreement dividing Arab provinces of Ottoman Empire between Britain and France.

June: Sharif Hussein proclaims Arab independence from Ottoman rule on basis of his correspondence with McMahon. Arab Revolt against Constantinople begins.

November: Sharif Hussein proclaimed "King of the Arab countries."

1917 November 2: British Foreign Secretary Arthur James Balfour sends letter to Baron Lionel Walter de Rothschild pledging British support for establishment of Jewish national home in Palestine (Balfour Declaration).

December 9: Surrender of Ottoman forces in Jerusalem to Allied forces under General Sir Edmund Allenby.

1918 September: Whole of Palestine occupied by Allied forces under General Allenby.

October 30: End of World War I.

Political and Public Events

"In the Name of God, Let Palestine Be Left Alone"

3, 3a, 3b Yusuf Diya-uddin Pasha al-Khalidi, elected from Jerusalem to the first Ottoman Parliament of 1877, where he was an active member of the opposition; mayor of Jerusalem in 1899. Elections to the Parliament were held immediately after the promulgation of the Constitution in 1876, but this first Ottoman Parliament was dissolved within a year of its election because the authorities feared the liberal attitudes of deputies like al-Khalidi. Also a scholar, al-Khalidi lectured at the University of Vienna and (while governor of a Kurdish province) wrote the first Arabic-Kurdish dictionary. In a letter to Zadok Kahn, the chief rabbi of France, he suggested that, since Palestine was already inhabited, the Zionists should find another place for the implementation of their political goals. ". . . in the name of God," he wrote, "let Palestine be left alone." Kahn showed the letter to Theodore Herzl, the founder of political Zionism. On 19 March 1899 Herzl replied to al-Khalidi in French (3a and 3b show the first and last pages of the letter) assuring him that, if the Zionists were not wanted in Palestine, "We will search and, believe me, we will find elsewhere what we need."

3

3a

3b

4

The Inauguration of a Hospital

4 Shaikh Badr, a western suburb of Jerusalem near the village of Deir Yassin (see 411). Those attending the ceremony include senior Ottoman officials, among them Palestinian Arabs (in formal dress on the porch), as well as other Palestinian notables and civil servants. First lower left is Elias Habib, the Christian Orthodox chief clerk of the Jerusalem municipality.

The Kaiser in Jerusalem

5 Kaiser Wilhelm II of Germany at the Mosque of the Dome of the Rock (see 1), Jerusalem, 1898. The Kaiser's visit was meant to signal to other European powers Germany's interest in the Arab East, and to strengthen German-Ottoman ties.

The "Young Turks" Revolution

6 The Grand Serai (see 164, 393), housing local government offices, Jaffa, July 1908: A large Palestinian crowd gathers to celebrate the revolution in Constantinople popularly known by the Arabs as al-Hurriyyah (Arabic for "liberty") and declared by the "Young Turks" against the despotic sultan Abdul Hamid. The revolution called for the restoration of the Constitution of 1876 and the holding of elections for a new Parliament (see 3). Both Arabs and Turks participated in the "Young Turks" movement but, as World War I approached, tensions between the two peoples mounted.

5

6

7

8

9

7 Jerusalem, 1908: A Palestinian rally, with local officials, celebrating al-Hurriyyah.

World War I and the Arab Revolt

8 Jemal Pasha, a member of the "Young Turks"
   triumvirate, which ruled the Ottoman Empire
   during World War I, with his staff in Jerusalem.
   Jemal Pasha became governor general and commander of the Ottoman Fourth Army in Syria-Palestine in 1914. After the initial stirrings of the
   Arab Revolt against the Turks, and on the side of
   Britain and the Allies, Jemal Pasha initiated a policy of brutal repression against Arab nationalists
   in Syria and Palestine. On 21 August 1915 and 6
   May 1916, he executed thirty-two leading Syrian
   and Palestinian intellectuals and professionals accused of being in favor of the Arab Revolt. The
   Arab Revolt aspired to the independence and political federation of the Arab countries, including
   Palestine, goals which the Arabs had been led to
   believe Britain and the Allies supported.

9 Jemal Pasha reviewing his troops in the western
   suburbs of Jerusalem, ca. 1917.

10

11

12

13

10, 11 Aqaba, 1917: Troops of the Arab Revolt.

12 The Jerusalem railroad station, 1917: Jemal Pasha,
Ottoman governor general in Syria-Palestine, and
General Erich von Falkenhayn, chief of the Ger-
man Military Mission to the Orient.

13 Jerusalem, 1917: German and Turkish staff officers.

14

General Allenby in Palestine

14 Jerusalem, 9 December 1917: British noncommissioned officers belonging to an advance party of the 219th Battalion, London Regiment, accepting the surrender of Jerusalem from Hussein Salim al-Husseini, mayor of Jerusalem (fourth right with cane). Second right is Ahmad Sharaf, a Palestinian police inspector.

15 The Citadel, Old City of Jerusalem, 11 December 1917: General Sir Edmund Allenby, commander in chief of the Allied Expeditionary Force, on the occasion of the proclamation of martial law after his entry into the city.

16 Allenby's proclamation: *". . . lest any of you should be alarmed. . . ."*

15

PROCLAMATION
OF MARTIAL LAW IN JERUSALEM.

To the inhabitants of Jerusalem the Blessed and the people dwelling in its vicinity.

The defeat inflicted upon the Turks by the troops under my command has resulted in the occupation of your City by my forces. I therefore here and now proclaim it to be under Martial Law, under which form of administration it will remain so long as military considerations make it necessary.

However, lest any of you should be alarmed by reason of your experiences at the hands of the enemy who has retired, I hereby inform you that it is my desire that every person should pursue his lawful business without fear of interruption. Furthermore, since your City is regarded with affection by the adherents of three of the great religions of mankind, and its soil has been consecrated by the prayers and pilgrimages of devout people of those three religions for many centuries, therefore do I make known to you that every sacred building, monument, holy spot, shrine, traditional site, endowment, pious bequest or customary place of prayer, of whatsoever form of the three religions, will be maintained and protected according to the existing customs and beliefs of those to whose faiths they are sacred.

December 1917. **EDMUND HENRY HYNMAN ALLENBY, General,**
Commander-in-Chief Egyptian Expeditionary Force.

PROCLAMATION
DE LA LOI MARTIALE A JÉRUSALEM.

Aux habitants de la sainte ville de Jérusalem et à la population des environs.

La défaite infligée aux Turcs par les troupes que je commande a abouti à l'occupation de votre Cité par mon armée. En conséquence, je la proclame d'ores et déjà sous le régime de la Loi Martiale, auquel elle demeurera soumise pour autant que les considérations militaires le rendront nécessaire.

Néanmoins, et afin qu'aucun de vous n'en conçoive quelque alarme du fait de vos expériences passées avec l'ennemi qui s'est retiré, je viens par la présente vous informer que mon désir est que chacun de vous poursuive son légitime travail sans crainte d'interruption.

De plus, considérant que votre ville jouit de l'affection des adhérents des trois grandes religions de l'humanité et qu'au cours de plusieurs siècles son sol a été consacré par les prières et les pèlerinages des pieux fidèles de ces trois religions, je proclame conséquemment que tout édifice sacré, monument, lieu saint, sanctuaire, site traditionnel, dotation, legs pieux ou endroit habituel de prière, relevant de n'importe laquelle des trois religions précitées, sera maintenu et protégé conformément aux coutumes existantes et aux croyances des personnes au regard de qui ces lieux sont sacrés.

Décembre 1917. **EDMUND HENRY HYNMAN ALLENBY, Général,**
Commandant en Chef la Force Expéditionnaire d'Egypte.

PROCLAMAZIONE
DI LEGGE MARZIALE IN GERUSALEMME.

Agli abitanti di Gerusalemme la Sacra ed alla popolazione che vive nella sua vicinità.

La disfatta inflitta ai Turchi dall'armata sotto il mio comando ha avuto per risultato l'occupazione della Città vostra dalle mie truppe. Io per conseguenza dichiaro e la pongo sotto la Legge Marziale, e sotto tale forma verrà amministrata per tanto tempo quale le considerazioni militari lo considereranno necessario.

Tuttavia, se mai certuni si fossero allarmati per l'esperienza avuta sotto le mani del nemico che si è ritirato, io vi informo che è il mio desiderio che ogni persona prosegua ai suoi lavori ed affari senza interruzione.

Inoltre, siccome la Città vostra è considerata con affezione dagli aderenti da tre delle grandi religioni dell'umanità, ed il suo suolo è stato consacrato dalle preghiere ed i pellegrinaggi dei devoti popoli di queste tre religioni da parecchi secoli, proclamo che qualunque edifizio sacro, monumento, luogo santo, reliquiario, sito tradizionale, dotazione o pio luogo di culto o abituale di preghiera, di qualsiasi delle tre religioni precitate, saranno mantenuti e protetti conformemente agli usi esistenti ed alle credenze delle persone per le quali questi luoghi sono sacri.

Dicembre 1917. **EDMUND HENRI HYNMAN ALLENBY, Generale,**
Commandante in Capo la Forza di Spedizione d'Egitto.

16

17

17 Troops of the Fifth Australian Light Horse Brigade, under Allenby's command, enter Nablus to establish Allied control, 21 September 1918.

18 Men of one of the French contingents under Allenby's command, the Fourth Regiment Chasseurs d'Afrique, enter the village of Anabta east of Tulkarm in central Palestine, late September 1918.

19 And Indian troops (the Jodhpore and Mysore Lancers, Fifteenth Imperial Service Cavalry Brigade) enter Haifa, 23 September 1918.

18

19

Rural, Urban, and Religious Life

Rural Scenes
20 Horseman overlooking the village of Askar east of Nablus, central Palestine.

20

21 Horseman overlooking the village of Daburiyyah on the slopes of Mount Tabor, Galilee.

22 Standing figure looking toward Marj Ibn Amer (the Plain of Jezreel).

23 Shepherds' Field as seen from Bethlehem. The village in the background is Beit Sahur. Note the terraces.

24 The village of Battir, southwest of Jerusalem.

21

22

23

24

25 A general view of Jenin, central Palestine. (Bonfils)[1]

26 The village of Ein Karim, west of Jerusalem. (Bonfils)

Palestinian Ecumenism

The Palestine countryside is dotted with religious monuments and shrines sacred to Judaism, Christianity, and Islam. Of all the Muslim peoples, Arab and non-Arab, the Palestinian Muslims have been the most attuned to and the most respectful of the Judaic and Christian traditions, if only because they inhabit a land that bears the unmistakable imprint of those two faiths.

27 The Christian monastery of Mar Saba, commemorating a Byzantine ascetic of this name who died in A.D. 531. The monastery is located in the wilderness southeast of Jerusalem. *Mar* is the Arabic word for "saint." Many Palestinian Muslim shrines honor Hebrew prophets and Christian saints. (See 28–30, 38, 180, 183, 207–208)

25

26

28

28 The Mosque of Nabi Samu'il (the prophet Samuel), just northwest of Jerusalem. (Bonfils)

29 The Muslim shrine at the traditional tomb of Nabi Yusuf (the prophet Joseph), east of Nablus.

30 The Muslim shrine at the traditional site of Tabitha's Well, east of Jaffa. Tabitha is mentioned in Acts 9:36-41.

29

30

Villagers of Central Palestine
31 A family in Ramallah, north of Jerusalem.

31

32

32 A group of villagers in Bethlehem, south of Jerusalem.

33 Bethlehem women at home drinking coffee and smoking a water pipe, or "hubble-bubble."

34 A Bonfils portrait of two young girls from Bethlehem. Each region in Palestine has its distinctive embroidery patterns and style for adorning women's clothing. The headdress often has coins sewn onto it.

35 An unidentified but typical village headman from the Jerusalem district. Note the sheepskin coat turned inward.

33

34   35

59

36

37

38

Cities and Towns

36 Auja al-Hafir, near the Egyptian border; in the foreground is the central square. Note the Ottoman army camps on the outskirts.

37 Gaza, "the City of Hashim"; so called because Gaza is the burial place of Hashim, grandfather of the prophet Muhammad. (Bonfils)

38 Hebron (al-Khalil in Arabic). The Arabic name means "friend" or "companion," the reference being to Abraham, the "friend" or "companion" of God, who is believed by Muslims as well as Jews to have been buried in Hebron. The minarets in the photograph are those of the Grand Mosque, built in honor of Abraham; Muslims revere him as the builder of the Ka'bah, the holiest of holies, in Mecca. (See 28–29, 180, 183, 207–208)

39 The Old City of Jerusalem (looking east toward the Mount of Olives) as seen from the belfry of the Church of St. Saviour. Note the Mosque of the Dome of the Rock, top right. (Bonfils)

39

843 - N°2 Panorama de Jerusalem pris du clocher St Sauveur

40

41

42

43

40, 41 Scenes at Jaffa Gate, the Old City of Jerusalem: (40) a Bonfils photograph taken just inside the walls looking out, and (41) the view from outside the walls.

42 Ramleh, from the west. Ramleh was founded by the Arabs in A.D. 716, and for some time thereafter it was the capital of the Arab province (*djund*) of Filastin (Palestine).

43 Jaffa, looking south. (Bonfils)

44 Jaffa, from the sea.

44

45

46

47

48

45 Jaffa: one of the first railroad piers to be built at the port.

46 Nablus and Mount Gerizim.

47 Haifa: a view of the Palestinian quarters from the northeast.

48 Haifa: a general view from Mount Carmel.

Jérusalem N° 1069 Mosquée El Aksa vue générale

49

50

52

51

Mosques, Churches, and Rites

49 The Mosque of al-Aqsa, Jerusalem (see 1), built by the caliph al-Walid ibn-Abd al-Malik (A.D. 705–715). Subsequently maintained and embellished by successive Arab and Muslim rulers, it has remained the focus of the pious attention of millions of Muslims throughout the world.

50 Interior of the Dome of the Rock (see 1).

51 The Dome of the Rock as seen from the al-Aqsa Mosque. In the foreground is al-Kas (the Cup), a fountain for ritual ablutions. (Bonfils)

52 Russian pilgrims at the Jordan River. Following the development of steamship navigation, the number of Christian pilgrims from Europe greatly increased.

53 Grotto of the Nativity, Church of the Nativity, Bethlehem (see 2). Note the Ottoman gendarme standing guard to prevent intersectarian Christian conflict.

54 Pilgrims entering the town of Bethlehem on Christmas Day. (Bonfils)

55 Jewish women praying at the Wailing Wall, Jerusalem. Throughout the centuries of Arab and Muslim rule in Palestine, Jews had free access to the Wailing Wall. Access became an issue only after the 1948 War and the resultant Palestinian diaspora. (See 90, 203)

56 The minaret of the White Mosque at Ramleh; also known as the Tower of the Forty Martyrs. Rebuilt in A.D. 1318, it was situated at the midpoint of the mosque enclosure's north wall. The mosque is otherwise in ruins. (Bonfils)

53

54

55

56

57

57 The Crusader church of St. Anne in the Old City of Jerusalem, built in A.D. 1140. The Ottoman governor gave the church to France in 1856, hence the tricolor French flag. (Bonfils)

58 Christian Orthodox procession on Easter Day (note the lighted candles) from the Greek Patriarchate to the Holy Sepulcher in the Old City of Jerusalem, ca. 1910.

Schools, Libraries, and Sports

59 A soccer match in the Palestinian quarter of Bab al-Zahirah (Herod's Gate), outside the Old City walls to the northeast — perhaps the earliest photograph of a sports event in Jerusalem. Note the Muslim tomb in the foreground, extreme right.

60 Staff and students of the Christian Orthodox Girls' School in Beit Jala (near Bethlehem), 1906. Note that the students are wearing their traditional costumes. The school was founded in Jerusalem in 1858 by a Russian benefactress, and subsequently maintained at the expense of Czarina Marya Aleksandrovna.

58

59

60

61 The Dusturiyyah (Constitutional) School, Jerusalem, 1909; named after the Ottoman Constitution promulgated in 1908 (see 3, 6–7). Its founder and headmaster, Khalil Sakakini (seated far left), was a distinguished Christian Orthodox Palestinian scholar and essayist. Established alongside state and Christian mission schools, the Dusturiyyah School stressed a secular curriculum and served as the prototype for private Palestinian schools.

61

62

62 St. George's British Anglican school for boys, founded in Jerusalem in 1899, was one of many schools established in the second half of the nineteenth century by European and American missionaries. Many of the students at St. George's came from Palestinian Protestant families, but boys from Muslim families increasingly attended St. George's and other Christian mission schools well before World War I. This photograph shows the staff and students of St. George's School in 1906. Standing far left is Shibli Jamal, a Palestinian Protestant who became a member of the First Palestinian Delegation to London in 1921, sent to explain the Palestinian point of view (see 84–86).

63 The St. George's player on the left is Izzat Tannous, a Protestant Palestinian who became a medical doctor and a representative of the Palestine Arab Higher Committee at the United Nations General Assembly. (This committee was the highest Palestinian political body during the British Mandate period; see 242.)

64 St. George's soccer team. One of its proudest feats was to beat the American University of Beirut's team on the latter's home ground in 1909. (See 231–232)

65 A corner of the Khalidi Library, Bab al-Silsilah (Gate of the Chain), the Old City of Jerusalem, ca. 1914. The library was established in 1900 through an endowment provided by the mother of Haj Raghib al-Khalidi (seated second from right). It was open to the public, and housed probably the largest single collection of medieval Arabic manuscripts in Palestine.

64

63

65

Portrait Gallery

66 Ruhi al-Khalidi (1861–1913), elected from Jerusalem to the Ottoman Parliament in 1908 and 1912, and vice-president of the Parliament in 1911. Earlier in his career he had lectured at the Sorbonne and served as Ottoman consul general in Bordeaux. A pioneer of modern Palestinian historiography, he wrote, among other works, *The Eastern Question, A Comparative Study of Arabic and French Literatures,* and one of the earliest treatises in Arabic on Zionism.

67 Faidi al-Alami, mayor of Jerusalem between 1906 and 1909, and Jerusalem representative in the Ottoman Parliament from 1914 to 1918. Alami was also a scholar, who published a concordance of the Koran. He was the father of Musa al-Alami, a distinguished Palestinian of the British Mandate period (see 343).

68 Arif Pasha Dajani (died 1930), mayor of Jerusalem during World War I. Immediately after the war he headed the Muslim-Christian Society in Jerusalem. Between 27 January and 10 February 1919, twenty-seven of these societies, which had been formed in different parts of the country, assembled in Jerusalem under his presidency to constitute the First Palestinian National Congress. The congress demanded an independent Palestinian government federated with Syria; it rejected Zionist political claims but offered equal rights to native Jews. This was the first of seven Palestinian national congresses that were held between 1919 and 1928 (see 78, 82–83, 87, 89).

69 Shaikh As'ad al-Shukairi, elected to the Ottoman Parliament from Acre in 1908 and 1912. He was trained in Islamic religious law, having graduated from Azhar University, Cairo. Shukairi occupied many positions in the Ottoman religious judiciary in Palestine and elsewhere, including that of president of the Court of Appeal for the Adana Province (Asia Minor). For a time he was librarian of the Imperial Library, Yildiz Palace, Istanbul, and during World War I served as mufti (interpreter of religious law) of the Fourth Ottoman Army in Syria-Palestine. He was the father of Ahmad Shukairi, who became chairman of the Palestine Liberation Organization (PLO) in 1964 (see 105, 224).

70 Nicola Abdo, an administrator in the Orthodox Patriarchate, Jerusalem.

66

67

68

69

70

71 Khalil Jawhariyyah was the brother of Wasif Jawhariyyah, a noted Christian Orthodox connoisseur, and the owner of one of the rich collections
of photographs widely used in this album. Khalil
is seen here in the uniform of a private in the Ottoman army during World War I. (See 201)

72 Khalil Raad, a famous Palestinian Protestant photographer from Jerusalem, and the owner of another of the collections used in this album. He
studied photography in Basel, and appears here in
his Ottoman army uniform during World War I.
(See 124–136)

73 Sa'id al-Shawwa, a leading Gaza notable and grain
exporter. After the British occupation, he became
mayor of Gaza and a member of the Supreme
Muslim Council — the highest body in charge of
Muslim community affairs. He represented Gaza
at the First, Fourth, and Fifth Palestinian National
Congresses held in 1919, 1921, and 1922, respectively (see 68, 82–83, 87).

74 Theodore Baramki, a Christian Orthodox Jerusalem judge, in formal Ottoman dress.

72

71

73

74

75 Saba Ya'qub Sa'id, a Christian Orthodox lawyer, and legal counselor to the Orthodox Patriarchate in Palestine.

76 George Humsi, a Christian Orthodox lawyer and author, Jerusalem.

77 Nazif al-Khalidi, a Jerusalem engineer. He was one of the principal aides to the German chief engineer Meissner, who supervised the building of the Hijaz Railway, begun in 1900; this railroad linked Damascus and Medina. Nazif Hill in present-day Amman is named after him because he camped on it with his staff during the construction of the railroad.

78 Musa Kazim Pasha al-Husseini, the elder statesman of Palestinian politics in the 1920s and early 1930s. A graduate of Maktab Mulkiye (Civil Service School) in Constantinople, he held important administrative positions in the Ottoman Empire. Between 1892 and 1913 he was *mutasarrif* ("governor") of several provinces in the Arabian Peninsula, Syria, and Asia Minor. Shortly after the British occupied Palestine, he was appointed mayor of Jerusalem, but was removed from office in April 1920 for his opposition to British pro-Zionist policies. From that date until his death in 1934, he led the Palestinian national movement (see 68, 84–86, 100–101, 104, 111–112). He was the father of Abd al-Qadir al-Husseini, who became a leader of the Palestinian resistance during the Great Rebellion of 1936–39 and again in the 1948 War (see 253, 396, 409–411).

76

75

77

PART II

FROM THE BRITISH OCCUPATION TO THE GREAT PALESTINE REBELLION

1918–1935

INTRODUCTION

THE end of World War I brought bitter disappointment and a pervasive sense of foreboding to the Palestinians, as news spread of the secret agreements between the Western powers and particularly of the Balfour Declaration. The Palestinians were terrified by the prospect of a Jewish national home in their country. This was what they had suspected to be the aim of Zionism since the 1880s, but in spite of its weakness the Ottoman government had itself, at least, been opposed to Zionism. Now the paramount imperial power in the world, Great Britain, had taken Zionism under its wing. The wording of the Balfour Declaration added insult to injury by referring to the Palestinians as the "non-Jewish communities," even though they constituted 92 percent of the population. The Palestinians categorically rejected the proposition that Jewish association with Palestine in biblical times gave contemporary European Zionists a political title that overrode the Palestinians' birthright to their ancestral homeland. They were outraged at the cynicism of Britain in giving their country to a third party. Their disillusionment and feeling of betrayal were all the greater because of Britain's wartime promises to Sharif Hussein and the Arab wartime alliance with Britain against Constantinople.

THE POSTWAR SETTLEMENT AND THE MANDATE SYSTEM

In June 1919 the Treaty of Versailles and the Covenant of the League of Nations were signed. The future of the Arab provinces of the Ottoman Empire was ostensibly to be governed by Article 22 of the covenant, emanating from the lofty Wilsonian principle of self-determination. Article 22 stipulated that the well-being of the Arab provinces was "a sacred trust of civilization." The communities inhabiting them were to be recognized as "independent nations" subject to the rendering of administrative assistance by a Mandatory. The wishes of the communities themselves would be "a principal consideration" in the selection of the Mandatory.

The Palestinians reacted to the Balfour Declaration and the proposed Mandate system by identifying themselves more closely with the pan-Arab national movement led by Sharif Hussein, whose son Emir (Prince) Faisal had installed himself in Damascus. In July 1919 Palestinian delegates attended a pan-Arab congress there at which Faisal was elected king of a state comprising Palestine, Lebanon, Transjordan, and Syria. Faisal's rule in Damascus was short-lived; by July 1920 he had been deposed by the French, who proceeded to impose their rule on Lebanon and Syria in accordance with an agreement made with Britain.

During 1919–20 the Palestinians pinned their hopes on the King-Crane Commission of Inquiry, dispatched in May 1919 by President Woodrow Wilson to ascertain the wishes of the region's inhabitants regarding their future. In August 1919 the commission reported on the depth of Palestinian fear of Zionism. Noting that the Zionists "looked forward to a practically complete dispossession of the present non-Jewish inhabitants of Palestine by various forms of purchase," they recommended serious modification of the Zionist program. Nothing came of the report, however, because of Wilson's disabling illness and the Senate's failure to endorse his signature on the Versailles treaty, which resulted in the disengagement of the United States from the postwar settlement. The following April riots broke out in Palestine, in which five Jews were killed and two hundred wounded. A British commission of inquiry attributed the riots to Palestinian "disap-

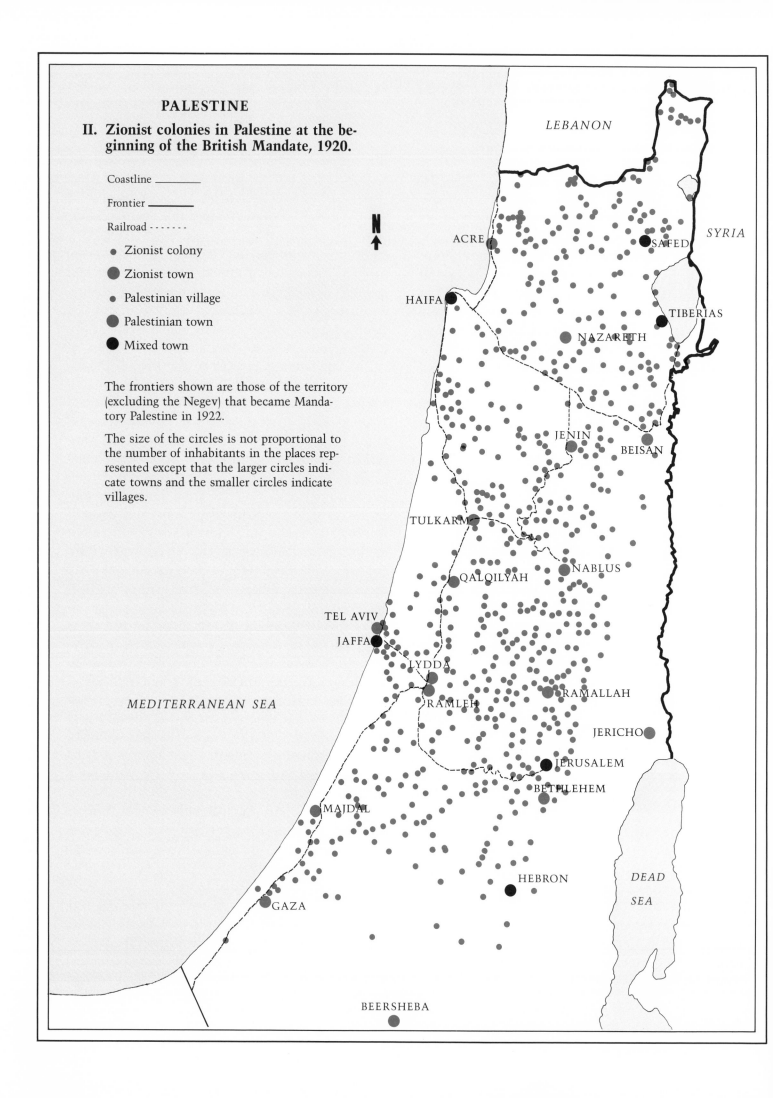

PALESTINE

II. Zionist colonies in Palestine at the beginning of the British Mandate, 1920.

Coastline ————

Frontier ————

Railroad - - - - - -

• Zionist colony

● Zionist town

• Palestinian village

● Palestinian town

● Mixed town

The frontiers shown are those of the territory (excluding the Negev) that became Mandatory Palestine in 1922.

The size of the circles is not proportional to the number of inhabitants in the places represented except that the larger circles indicate towns and the smaller circles indicate villages.

N

LEBANON

SYRIA

ACRE

HAIFA

SAFED

TIBERIAS

NAZARETH

JENIN

BEISAN

TULKARM

NABLUS

QALQILYAH

TEL AVIV

JAFFA

LYDDA

RAMLEH

RAMALLAH

JERICHO

JERUSALEM

BETHLEHEM

MEDITERRANEAN SEA

MAJDAL

HEBRON

DEAD

SEA

GAZA

BEERSHEBA

pointment at the non-fulfillment of the promise of independence" and "fear of economic and political subjection" to the Zionists.

Undeterred, the British proceeded forthwith to implement the Balfour Declaration while still in military occupation of the country and before their status there had been approved by the League of Nations. They inaugurated their regime by dismissing the Palestinian mayor of Jerusalem for opposing the Zionist program. The Mandate for Palestine was "allotted" to Britain in April 1920 by the Supreme Council of the Peace Conference at San Remo without any reference to the wishes of the Palestinians. In July the British appointed Sir Herbert Samuel, an avowed Zionist, as first high commissioner of a new civilian administration. Without Palestinian consent, Samuel announced in August a quota of 16,500 Jewish immigrants for his first year in office. In May 1921 Palestinian protests against Zionist mass immigration resulted in new riots, in which 46 Jews were killed and 146 wounded. Another British commission of inquiry confirmed that fear of the consequences of Zionist immigration was the reason for the disturbances.

Meanwhile, the Palestinians had begun to organize themselves. Christian-Muslim associations were formed throughout the country. These associations in turn elected delegates to a national congress, which elected an Executive Committee. Three national congresses were held between January 1919 and August 1922. All three congresses expressed fear of Zionist political objectives and rejected the Balfour Declaration. Demanding the cessation of Zionist mass immigration and of the transfer of Palestinian land to Zionist ownership, they called for a government on the basis of proportional representation. In 1921 and 1922 the Palestinians also sent three delegations to London to present their case.

In 1922 the British government issued a White Paper (statement of policy) explaining its objectives in Palestine: The intention was not that Palestine as a whole should be converted into a Jewish national home, but that such a home should be established *in* Palestine; Jewish immigration would continue and be regulated by "the economic absorptive capacity" of the country; Transjordan would lie outside the scope of the

Balfour Declaration. The Palestinians rejected the 1922 White Paper because Zionist mass immigration, which had a declared political objective, would be regulated solely by economic criteria — the very reason why the Zionist leadership accepted it.

The terms of the Mandate were approved by the League of Nations Council in July 1922 without the consent of the Palestinians. Article 2 made the Mandatory responsible for placing the country under such "political, administrative, and economic conditions as [would] secure the establishment of the Jewish national home . . . and the development of self-governing institutions." Article 4 allowed for the establishment of a Jewish agency, representing the Jews of the world, to advise the Mandatory. Article 6 stipulated that the Mandatory, "while ensuring that the rights and position of other sections of the population [were] not prejudiced, [should] facilitate Jewish immigration under suitable conditions . . . and close settlement by the Jews on the land."

The Mandate as a whole was seen by the Palestinians as an Anglo-Zionist condominium and its terms as instruments for the implementation of the Zionist program; it had been imposed on them by force, and they considered it to be both morally and legally invalid. But the isolation of the Palestinians was complete inasmuch as all the neighboring Arab countries had themselves recently fallen under foreign occupation — Lebanon and Syria under the French, and Transjordan and Iraq under the British (Egypt had been under British occupation since 1882). The one factor that favored the Palestinians was the status quo in regard to the demography and ownership of the country: The Palestinians constituted the vast majority of the population and owned the bulk of the land. Inevitably the ensuing struggle centered on this status quo. The British and the Zionists were determined to subvert and revolutionize it, the Palestinians to defend and preserve it; hence the Palestinians' instinctive and persistent feeling that they were on the defensive, reacting to the actions and designs of their opponents. The main issues of conflict concerned mass immigration, land transfer, and representative government. The Zionists and the British clearly aimed at using mass immigration to change the demographic balance between Zionist immigrants and Palestinian residents, and land transfer to change the landownership balance between the two groups. The Palestinians' only hope lay in the application of representative government. But neither the British nor the Zionists at any time during the Mandate accepted the democratic principle as applicable to Palestine, because its observance would have entailed acknowledging the presence of a Palestinian majority, which would have prejudiced the development of the Jewish national home.

The years between 1923 and 1929 were relatively quiet, with a dramatic decline in Zionist immigration occurring in 1927–28. But the Jewish national home continued to grow. From 1918 to 1929 some sixty new Zionist colonies were established, Zionist landownership rose from 2.04 percent of the total area of the country (in 1919) to 4.4 percent (in 1929), and the proportion of the Jewish population rose (largely through mass immigration) from 9.7 percent to 17.6 percent during the same period.

MOUNTING PALESTINIAN FEARS

The pent-up feelings of the Palestinians were released by two contemporaneous events. In August 1929 the Jewish Agency (envisaged in the Mandate), representing all the Jewish communities in the world and including both Zionists and non-Zionists, was created. The appearance of some world-famous Jewish figures as members of the Jewish Agency increased Palestinian fears of Zionist political influence on Britain. The other event was an unprovoked and unprecedented political demonstration held at the Wailing Wall adjacent to the Muslim Haram al-Sharif (Noble Sanctuary). The demonstrators were militant right-wing secular members of the Zionist Revisionist Party, so called because it advocated the "revision" of the Mandate to include the forcible colonization of Transjordan in addition to Palestine. (This party had been founded in 1925 by the Polish Zionist Vladimir Jabotinsky.) The demonstration was perceived as evidence of Zionist designs on the mosques of the Dome of the Rock and al-Aqsa inside the sanctuary, and gave rise to violent clashes in which 133 Jews were killed and 339 wounded.

In March 1930 the report of a British commission of inquiry attributed the 1929 clashes to the fact that the Palestinians "have come to see in Jewish immigration not only a menace to their livelihood but a possible overlord of the future." Another report, issued in October by a British expert, established that there was no additional land available for agricultural settlement by new Zionist immigrants. The British government immediately issued a White Paper that took cognizance of the findings of these two reports and advocated greater attentiveness to Palestinian grievances. Not unexpectedly, the Zionist leadership fiercely criticized the 1930 White Paper, fearing that a British policy of evenhandedness would militate against the achievement of Zionist goals. Bowing to Zionist pressure, the British government virtually withdrew the White Paper in February 1931 and dispatched to Palestine a new high commissioner, General Sir Arthur Wauchope, with instructions to accelerate the development of the Jewish national home.

The retraction of the 1930 White Paper convinced the Palestinians that there could be no legal redress of their grievances, and that expert recommendations based on direct knowledge of the facts and merits of their case could always be annulled by the exercise of Zionist political leverage at the center of power in London. In December 1931 a Muslim congress held in Jerusalem and attended by delegates from twenty-two Muslim states warned against the political dangers of British pro-Zionist policies. Unconcerned, the British replied by sponsoring Zionist mass immigration (mostly from Poland) in ever-larger numbers. Between 1931 and 1936, sixty-four more Zionist colonies were established, Zionist landownership rose from 4.5 percent to 5.4 percent of the total area of the country, and the proportion of the Jewish population rose (largely through immigration) from 17.8 percent to 29.5 percent.

The escalating rate of immigration (30,000 in 1933, 42,000 in 1934, and 61,000 in 1935) was what finally produced panic and desperation among the Palestinians. The massive convergence on Palestine of Jewish immigrants was, of course, a result of the serious deterioration of living conditions for Jews in many European countries. It was also a result of the Zionists' deliberate channeling of Jewish immigration toward Palestine to the exclusion of other countries of possible refuge with much greater absorptive capacities. This Zionist policy played into the hands of powerful conservative elements in the United States and the British dominions, who felt absolved of any moral obligation to liberalize their own immigration legislation so as to allow the reception of substantial numbers of Jewish refugees. It also caused the Jewish leadership in these countries to conform to Zionist preferences and refrain from exerting any pressure on their own governments in the direction of liberalization. Thus Zionist pre–World War II immigration policies in effect kept the doors of the United States and the British dominions virtually closed to large-scale Jewish immigration, and thereby drastically reduced the number of Jews who could have left Europe before it was too late. Paradoxically, the opposition on religious grounds (particularly in Poland) of the mainstream Jewish religious leadership to Jewish emigration under Zionist auspices further inhibited prewar Jewish emigration from Europe, even to Palestine.[1]

The leadership of the Palestinian national movement had passed in 1933 to Haj Amin al-Husseini, mufti (highest Muslim dignitary) of Jerusalem. Haj Amin was coming under increasing pressure from both popular mass sentiment and the intelligentsia for his failure to stand up to the British. The political restlessness of the country was reflected in the rapid formation of five new Palestinian political parties during the period from 1932 to 1935. A general consensus was emerging that political and diplomatic efforts were ineffective and only an armed rebellion directed at Britain could yield results. An early expression of this view led to the death in action against the British, in November 1935, of a Muslim preacher and reformer from Haifa named Izz al-Din al-Qassam, together with his comrades. Theirs was the first Palestinian guerrilla operation, and al-Qassam and his comrades became national martyrs overnight.

In December 1935 in a last-minute attempt to allay Palestinian fears, the British administration in Palestine suggested the formation of a local Legislative Council composed of twenty-eight members, fourteen of whom would be Palestinians. Although the Palestinians then constituted 70.5 percent of the total population, they were willing in their despair to accept the proposal. But when the British House of Commons proceeded to debate the matter, the government was forced to withdraw the Legislative Council proposal because of vehement attacks by pro-Zionist members of Parliament, who argued that it would hinder the development of the Jewish national home. For the Palestinians this was final confirmation, if any were needed, that there could be no appeal, in their case, to the British sense of fair play.

CHRONOLOGY

1919 January: Paris Peace Conference decides conquered Arab provinces will not be restored to Ottoman rule.

January 27–February 10: First Palestinian National Congress, meeting in Jerusalem, sends to peace conference two memoranda rejecting Balfour Declaration and demanding independence.

March 25: Peace conference decides to send international commission of inquiry to ascertain aspirations of Near East peoples.

June–July: Henry C. King and Charles R. Crane, U.S. members of international commission of inquiry, proceed to Near East alone after failure of Britain and France to join commission.

June 28: Treaty of Versailles and League of Nations Covenant signed.

July 2: General Syrian Congress, held in Damascus and attended by Palestinian delegates, announces its rejection of Balfour Declaration.

August 28: Report of King-Crane Commission of Inquiry, submitted to Paris Peace Conference, recommends that "the project for making Palestine distinctly a Jewish commonwealth should be given up."

1920 March: General Syrian Congress proclaims independence of Syria, Lebanon, Palestine, and Transjordan, with Prince Faisal as king.

April: Disturbances break out in Palestine due to fears of Zionism and nonfulfillment of promises of independence; five Jews killed and 200 wounded. British appoint Palin Commission of Inquiry.

British remove Musa Kazim Pasha al-Husseini, mayor of Jerusalem, from office for opposing their pro-Zionist policies.

April 25: Supreme Council of San Remo Peace Conference assigns Palestine Mandate to Britain without consent of Palestinians.

May: British prevent Second Palestinian National Congress from convening.

July 1: British civilian administration inaugurated; Sir Herbert Samuel appointed first high commissioner.

August 26: First Immigration Ordinance sets quota of 16,500 Jewish immigrants for first year.

December: Third Palestinian National Congress, meeting in Haifa, elects Executive Committee, which remains in control of Palestinian political movement from 1920 to 1935.

1921 May–June: Fourth Palestinian National Congress, convening in Jerusalem, decides to send Palestinian delegation to London to explain Palestinian case against Balfour Declaration.

Syrian-Palestinian Conference held in Geneva.

May 1: Outbreak of disturbances in Jaffa protesting Zionist mass immigration; 46 Jews killed and 146 wounded.

May 8: Haj Amin al-Husseini appointed mufti (highest Muslim religious dignitary) of Jerusalem.

October: Haycraft Commission of Inquiry attributes Jaffa disturbances to Palestinian fears of steadily increasing Zionist mass immigration.

1922 February: Second Palestinian Delegation to London announces its rejection of Balfour Declaration to British Colonial Secretary Winston Churchill, and demands national independence.

June 3: Churchill issues White Paper of 1922 on Palestine interpreting British concept of Jewish "national home," and excluding Transjordan from scope of Balfour Declaration.

June 30: U.S. Congress endorses Balfour Declaration.

July 24: League of Nations Council approves Mandate for Palestine without consent of Palestinians.

August: Fifth Palestinian National Congress, meeting in Nablus, agrees to economic boycott of Zionists. (See 1901 entry on Keren Kayemeth.)

October: First British census of Palestine shows total population of 757,182, with 78 percent Muslim, 11 percent Jewish, and 9.6 percent Christian.

1923 January: Resigning from Zionist Executive, Polish Zionist leader Vladimir Jabotinsky calls for forcible colonization of Palestine and Transjordan.

September 29: British Mandate for Palestine comes officially into force.

1925 Jabotinsky forms Revisionist Party with aim of "revising" Mandate to include colonization of Transjordan.

March: Palestinian general strike protests private visit by Lord Balfour to Jerusalem.

October: Sixth Palestinian National Congress convenes in Jaffa.

1928 June: Seventh Palestinian National Congress convenes in Jerusalem.

September 24: First attempt by some Jewish religious leaders to change "status quo" at Wailing Wall.

November: Islamic Conference, meeting in Jerusalem, demands protection of Muslim property rights at Wailing Wall, itself a Muslim holy site.

1929 August 15: First political demonstration by militant Zionist groups at Wailing Wall.

August 23–29: Palestinians riot in several towns in reaction to militant demonstrations at Wailing Wall. In resulting clashes, 133 Jews killed and 339 wounded; 116 Palestinians killed and 232 wounded, mostly at hands of British military.

October: General conference convenes in Jerusalem to formulate Palestinian position on Wailing Wall controversy.

1930 January 14: League of Nations Council appoints international commission to investigate legal status of Palestinians and Jews at Wailing Wall.

March: British-appointed Shaw Commission of Inquiry reports on 1929 disturbances; it attributes causes to fact that "the Arabs have come to see in Jewish immigration not only a menace to their livelihood but a possible overlord of the future."

March 30: Fourth Palestinian Delegation arrives in London.

May: Fourth Palestinian Delegation to London announces British rejection of its demands for (1) cessation of Zionist mass immigration to and land acquisition in Palestine, and (2) establishment of democratic, representative government.

August 6: Jewish Agency for Palestine, enlarged in 1929 to include Zionist and prominent non-Zionist Jewish leaders from various countries, recognized by Britain.

October: Sir John Hope-Simpson, appointed to inquire into problems of land settlement, immigration, and development in Palestine, reports there is no room for substantial number of Jewish settlers on the land.

British Colonial Secretary Lord Passfield (Sidney Webb) issues White Paper of 1930 on Palestine, which takes note of views expressed by Hope-Simpson and Shaw commissions of inquiry.

December: International Wailing Wall Commission recommends restoration of status quo ante, and confirms Muslim property rights at Wailing Wall.

1931 February 14: In letter to Chaim Weizmann, Prime Minister Ramsay MacDonald virtually retracts Lord Passfield's White Paper of 1930.

October: General Sir Arthur Wauchope succeeds Sir John Chancellor as high commissioner.

November 18: Second British census of Palestine shows total population of 1,035,154, with 73.4 percent Muslim, 16.9 percent Jewish, and 8.6 percent Christian.

December: Lewis French, British director of development for Palestine, publishes report on "landless Arabs."

December 16: Pan-Islamic Congress held in Jerusalem and attended by 145 delegates from all parts of Muslim world.

1932 August 2: Formation of Istiqlal (Independence) Party as first regularly constituted Palestinian political party.

1933 March: Arab Executive Committee (see December 1920) declares Zionist mass immigration "has terrified the country."

July 14: British secretary of state issues statement on resettlement of Palestinian tenant farmers displaced from land acquired by Zionists.

October: Arab Executive Committee calls for general strike to protest British pro-Zionist policies, especially sponsorship of Zionist mass immigration; disturbances break out in main towns.

1934 February: Special commission of inquiry under Sir William Murison reports on causes of 1933 disturbances.

December 2: Defense Party founded.

1935 March 27: Palestine Arab Party founded.

June 23: Reform Party founded.

October 5: National Bloc Party founded. Together with Istiqlal Party these four parties become principal Palestinian political parties.

October: Revisionists quit World Zionist Organization to form New Zionist Organization, with aim of forcibly "liberating" Palestine and Transjordan.

Irgun Zvai Leumi (National Military Organization) founded by dissident members of Haganah; Jabotinsky named commander in chief.

Large quantity of arms smuggled from Belgium by Zionist groups, discovered at Jaffa port.

November: Shaikh Izz al-Din al-Qassam, leading first Palestinian guerrilla group, dies in action against British security forces.

November 25: Leaders of Palestinian political parties submit joint memorandum to British high commissioner requesting cessation of Zionist mass immigration and land acquisition, and establishment of government on basis of proportional representation.

December 21–22: High commissioner proposes establishment of 28-member Legislative Council with Palestinians holding only 14 seats. Palestinians accept proposal in principle.

1936 March 25: Legislative Council proposal defeated by pro-Zionist members in British House of Commons.

79

The First Days of British Rule

79 Jaffa, June 1920: Sir Herbert Samuel (in white peaked helmet), a British Zionist politician appointed as first high commissioner, about to set foot on Palestinian soil to inaugurate the British civilian administration. This administration replaced the military administration that had been in force since General Allenby's arrival in Jerusalem (see 15–16). The letters on the vests of the boatmen, *OETA* (Occupied Enemy Territory Administration), denote the official designation of the military administration in Syria-Palestine. When followed by the letter *S* (for "South"), as in this case, the reference was to Palestine. *W* (for "West") and *E* (for "East") referred to Lebanon and Syria (including Transjordan), respectively.

80, 81 Jerusalem, April 1920. Indian troopers in the
British army evenhandedly search a Muslim dignitary (80) and a Christian priest (81).

80

81

Palestinian Political Organization

82 The Third Palestinian National Congress, Haifa, 14 December 1920. Delegates to the congress represented the main cities and districts of Palestine. Seven congresses were held between 1919 and 1928 (photographs of the First and Seventh Congresses are unavailable, and the British prevented the convening of the Second Congress, scheduled for May 1920; see 68). At the Third Congress it was decided to form an Executive Committee to conduct business between congresses. Musa Kazim Pasha al-Husseini (see 78) was chosen chairman of the committee and president of the congresses, posts he held until his death. These congresses, forerunners of the Palestinian National Congress (PNC) held under the aegis of the Palestine Liberation Organization (PLO) since 1964, reflect early Palestinian attempts at political organization. They passed resolutions expressing fear of Zionist objectives and affirming Palestinian demands for proportional representation and national independence. From right to left, the banner in Arabic reads: "Palestine is the cradle of Jesus"; "Preserve al-Aqsa Mosque"; "Palestine is Arab." Third right, last row, is the future Palestinian leader Haj Amin al-Husseini (see 88, 100, 202, 290) a few months before he became mufti (interpreter of religious law) of Jerusalem in May 1921.

83 The Fourth Palestinian National Congress, Jerusalem, 25 May 1921. (See 87, 89)

82

83

95

84

85

86

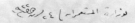

THE PALESTINE ARAB DELEGATION.

PRESIDENT: MOUSA KAZIM PASHA EL-HUSSEINI.
VICE-PRESIDENT: HAJJ TEWFIK HAMMAD.
SECRETARY: MI'SHIBLY JAMAL.
MEMBERS: MOUIN BEY EL-MADI.
AMIN BEY EL-TAMIMI.
IBRAHIM EFFENDI SHAMMAS.

HÔTEL CECIL,
LONDON, W.C.

24th. Oct., 1921.

The Rt. Hon. Winston Churchill, M.P.,
Colonial Secretary

Sir,

On behalf of the People of Palestine, whom we represent, we thank you for the opportunities which you have given us of stating their case to you.

We wish now to put before you briefly the salient points of the case, the presentation of which to the British Government was confided to us, and we request you to put it before the Cabinet and inform us of its views. We wish to impress upon you two points. First, that the case we put forward is supported by 93% of the people of Palestine, and second, that the People of Palestine will endorse a settlement of their present grievances on the lines we now suggest.

(1) The People of Palestine welcomed the victorious British troops believing that they had come to fulfil promises made to them during the war, and to safeguard their existence as a people and their right of self determination. The very serious and growing unrest among the Palestinians arises from their absolute conviction that the present policy of the British Government is directed towards evicting them from

86a

86b

detrimental to the Palestine people, this policy should be regulated, not in the interests of the Zionists, but of Palestinians.

We venture to point out, with all deference to you, Sir, that the people of Palestine will not be satisfied with promises that some control of their own destinies will be given to them in the future, while the Administration in the present allows their country to be subjected to a flood of alien immigration, and to be put largely under Zionist control.

The Palestine people will never admit the right of any outside organisation to dispossess them of their country, and to threaten their very existence as a people economically and politically.

We ask you, Sir, to put our views as herein set out before the Cabinet, to which we have sent a copy of this proposal. These views are, in the main, favourable, we could discuss with His Majesty's Government the details of the scheme subsequently to be submitted to the people of Palestine.

We are, Sir,

Yours faithfully,

Palestinian Diplomacy

84 The First Palestinian Delegation to the United Kingdom in working session in London, 1921. Two of the six-man delegation (first and fourth left) were Christian Palestinians. The delegation was elected by the Fourth Palestinian National Congress (see 83). Third left is Musa Kazim Pasha al-Husseini (see 78); fourth left is Shibli Jamal (see 62). This was the first of four Palestinian delegations to London undertaken during the period 1921–30 to explain Arab fears of the consequences of Zionist policies in Palestine.

85 The First Delegation at the Vatican en route to London.

86 The First Delegation in Geneva to attend the Syrian-Palestinian Conference, timed to coincide with the League of Nations' meeting to discuss the proposed Mandatory system. Members of the delegation are seen here with Syrian and Lebanese nationalists, many of whom had been exiled by French authorities. Michel Lutfallah (tall figure, front center), a Christian Lebanese nationalist, presided at the conference. First right, last row, is Riyad al-Sulh, prime minister of independent Lebanon in the 1940s. The conference demanded the independence and federation of Syria, Lebanon, and Palestine.

86a, 86b *". . . the people of Palestine will not be satisfied with promises that some control of their own destinies will be given to them in the future, . . . The Palestine people will never admit the right of any outside organization to dispossess them of their country, . . ."* Copies of the first and last pages of the memorandum submitted to Winston Churchill, British colonial secretary, by the First Palestinian Delegation to London, 24 October 1921.

من اوراق اكرم زعيتر

المؤتمر الخامس في نابلس في ٢٢ اغسطس ٩٢٢

87

. . . And Further Political Activity

87 The Fifth Palestinian National Congress, Nablus, August 1922 (see 68, 82–83, 89).

88 Jaffa Harbor, 1925. Haj Amin al-Husseini (see 82), now mufti of Jerusalem and president of the Supreme Muslim Council, the highest governing body for Muslim community affairs, confers with King Faisal I of Iraq, a leader of the Arab Revolt during World War I (see 8–11, 99, 106). Faisal was traveling by sea to France via Palestine. The Palestinians looked to him for support in their resistance to British pro-Zionist policies.

89 The Sixth Palestinian National Congress, Jaffa, October 1925 (see 68, 82–83, 87).

88

89

The 1929 Disturbances

90 The Arab commercial center outside Jaffa Gate, Jerusalem, on strike during the Buraq (Wailing Wall) disturbances, 1929. The Wailing Wall constitutes part of the western wall of the compound containing the mosques of the Dome of the Rock and al-Aqsa (see 1). Jewish access to the Wailing Wall (see 55) had for centuries been regulated by cumulative customary observances and procedures known as the "status quo," which were mutually acceptable to Jews and Muslims. An attempt by some Jewish religious leaders in September 1928 to change the status quo unilaterally was followed in August 1929 by an unprecedented political demonstration at the Wailing Wall, organized by militant right-wing Zionists. In the context of mounting Palestinian-Jewish tension, this incident touched off countrywide disturbances in which many Jews and Palestinians were killed, the latter mostly at the hands of the British.

91 British show of force, Jerusalem, August 1929.

90

91

92   The Emergency Relief Committee (seen here in session at its headquarters in Jerusalem, 1929) was formed during the 1929 disturbances to aid afflicted Palestinian families. Third right is Subhi al-Khadra, representative of the town of Safed (in Galilee), who later became one of the founders of the pan-Arab Istiqlal (Independence) Party (see 102, 105). Fourth right is Abd al-Hamid Shoman, founder of the Arab Bank. The Arab Bank, which established branches in all the major towns of Palestine and in the capitals of neighboring Arab countries, became the most successful and prestigious private Arab banking institution throughout the Arab world (see 289).

93   A delegation of Palestinian women outside the high commissioner's residence in Jerusalem. The delegation protested the harshness of British measures against the Palestinians during the disturbances. The women wearing hats are Christian. Second left is Mrs. Matiel Moghannam, a Protestant Palestinian feminist leader and author of *The Arab Woman and the Palestine Problem* (London: H. Joseph, 1937). Note the different degrees of veiling worn by the Muslim women — all city dwellers. By contrast, rural Muslim women wear no veils at all.

92

93

94

95

94 The motorcade of the women's delegation on its way to the high commissioner's residence.

The Shaw Commission of Inquiry:
"disappointment . . . and fear"

95 Members of the Shaw Commission of Inquiry, Jerusalem, October 1929. The Shaw Commission was sent by London to investigate the causes of the 1929 disturbances. Seated center is Sir Walter Shaw, chairman of the commission. In its report the commission concluded that the fundamental cause of the 1929 outbreak was the Palestinians' feeling of "disappointment of their political and national aspirations and fear for their economic future." It recommended that British policies on Zionist mass immigration to and land acquisition in Palestine should give due consideration to Palestinian interests and grievances.

Mourning on Balfour Day

96, 97 Balfour Day, the Old City of Jerusalem, 2 November 1929. Palestinians and many Arabs commemorated the anniversary of the Balfour Declaration (2 November 1917) with mourning, as indicated by the black flags. The person second left in 96 is carrying a collection box on behalf of the Emergency Relief Committee (see 92). The sash across his chest reads, "Honor thy martyrs."

96

97

98

99

Jerusalem: The Last Abode

Because of the special religious and historical significance of Jerusalem in Muslim eyes (see 1), many Muslim leaders from Arab and Muslim countries outside Palestine willed that Jerusalem be their burial place.

98 The funeral procession of Muhammad Ali, one of the foremost Indian Muslim religious leaders and scholars, escorted by Boy Scouts, Jerusalem, 23 January 1931.

99 The funeral of King Hussein of Hijaz, Jerusalem, 4 June 1931. Leader of the Arab Revolt during World War I (see 8–11), he was the father of King Faisal of Iraq (see 88, 106) and the great-grandfather of King Hussein of Jordan. It was to King Hussein of Hijaz that Britain had promised Arab independence, including that of Palestine, before issuing the Balfour Declaration.

Both men were buried in the precincts of the Haram al-Sharif (Noble Sanctuary), the compound that encloses the mosques of the Dome of the Rock (partly visible in 99) and al-Aqsa (see 1).

100

101

Continued Palestinian Diplomacy

100 A Palestinian conference called on the eve of the departure of the Fourth Palestinian Delegation to London; Jerusalem, March 1930 (see 84). The First Delegation to London in 1921 was followed by two others in 1922. The members of the Fourth Delegation (front row, left to right) were Awni Abd al-Hadi (see 196, 291), lawyer, pan-Arabist, and later a founder of the Istiqlal (Independence) Party (see 102, 105), who had been private secretary to King Faisal I (see 88, 106) at the Versailles Peace Conference in 1919; Haj

Amin al-Husseini, mufti of Jerusalem (see 82); Musa Kazim Pasha al-Husseini, chairman of the delegation (see 78); Raghib al-Nashashibi, mayor of Jerusalem (see 196, 242, 352); and Alfred Roch, prominent Catholic businessman from Jaffa (see 200, 242, 291).

101 Members of the Fourth Palestinian Delegation in London, April 1930. The women in the back row are Christian Palestinian secretaries accompanying the delegation. The three men in the same row are Palestinian correspondents in London for Arabic newspapers in Palestine.

102

103

الاجتماع العام الذي عقد في روضة المعارف للمؤتمر الاسلامي العام سنة ١٩٣١

The Rise of Political Activism

102 Young political activists from Nablus just released from prison (ca. 1930) call on their lawyer,
Adil Zu'aiter (seated), to thank him for his efforts on their behalf. The group is typical of a
rising middle-class generation that was increasingly critical of the Palestinian leadership's exclusive reliance on diplomacy. Most of these
men joined the Istiqlal (Independence) Party (see
100, 105). In addition to his legal practice,
Zu'aiter was a prolific translator from French
into Arabic; he translated works of Rousseau,
Voltaire, Anatole France, Montesquieu, and La-
martine (see 358).

The Jewish Agency and Pan-Islamic Reaction

103 The Pan-Islamic Conference, Jerusalem, December 1931. The formation in 1929 of the enlarged
Jewish Agency (to include many eminent and in-
fluential Zionist and non-Zionist Jewish leaders
from all over the world), and the perceived dan-
ger to the Muslim holy places in Jerusalem aris-
ing from tensions at the Wailing Wall (see 1, 90),
brought about a worldwide Islamic reaction. In
response to an invitation issued by Haj Amin al-
Husseini, mufti of Jerusalem, 145 delegates from
22 Islamic countries attended the Pan-Islamic
Conference. The conference voiced fears of right-
wing Zionist encroachment on the Muslim holy
places, and endorsed Palestinian demands for national independence.

104 Tunisian and Turkish delegates to the Pan-Islamic Conference with Musa Kazim Pasha al-
Husseini (see 78). First left is the Tunisian
scholar Abd al-Aziz al-Tha'alibi; the figure in the
center is the Turkish philosopher Rida Tawfiq.

Pan-Arabism

105 Members of the Istiqlal (Independence) Pan-Arab
Party, founded in 1932. Identifying British "imperialism" as the major foe because of its sponsorship of Zionism, the Istiqlal Party urged the
Palestinian leadership to concentrate its efforts
on resisting and terminating the British occupation (see 102). Standing first left is Ahmad Shukairi from Acre (see 69, 224), who became
chairman of the Palestine Liberation Organization (PLO) in 1964. Seated second left is Rashid
al-Haj Ibrahim from Haifa (see 268). Seated center is Muhammad Izzat Darwazah, author of a
classic history of the Arab national movement,
and a principal organizer of the Great Palestine
Rebellion of 1936–39 (see 242ff.).

106 The funeral cortege of King Faisal I of Iraq passing through Haifa, 1933. The king had died on a
visit to Europe, and his body was en route to
Iraq. The size of the crowd indicates the extent
of his popularity among the Palestinians, and the
hopes they pinned on Iraq's support in their resistance to British pro-Zionist policies. (See 88,
99)

104

105

106

107

108

109

Stirrings of Revolt against British Pro-Zionist Policies

The greatest single source of Palestinian fear for the future was British sponsorship of mounting Zionist mass immigration. Annual Jewish immigration rose from 4,075 (1931) to 9,553 (1932) to 30,327 (1933) to 42,359 (1934) to 61,854 (1935). The largest number of immigrants during this period came from Poland.

107 The aftermath of a Palestinian demonstration protesting Zionist mass immigration, New Gate, Jerusalem, 1933.

108 Aerial show of force by the British over the walls of the Old City of Jerusalem, 1933.

109 British riot police, mounted and on foot, block the path of a demonstration protesting Zionist mass immigration, Jaffa, 27 October 1933.

110 British mounted police charge into a crowd of demonstrators, Central Square, Jaffa, 27 October 1933.

111 The bearded profile of a fallen man in the upper center of the photograph is that of the venerable Musa Kazim Pasha al-Husseini (see 78), who had been leading the demonstration shown above (see 109–110). His aides are trying to shield him from the truncheons of British police officers.

110

111

112

113

112 The funeral of Musa Kazim Pasha al-Husseini, Damascus Gate, Jerusalem, 27 March 1934. Al-Husseini died at the age of eighty-one. The trauma he had suffered at the hands of the British five months earlier in Jaffa (see 111) hastened his death.

First Palestinian Guerrilla Operation

113 Shaikh Izz al-Din al-Qassam, patriot, social reformer, and religious teacher from Haifa. His work and preaching were conducted mainly among the poorer classes. Right-wing Zionist political demonstrations at the Wailing Wall (see 1, 90), the formation of the enlarged Jewish Agency (see 103), and British sponsorship of mounting Zionist mass immigration convinced him that political and diplomatic efforts were futile and only armed struggle against the British would influence London. In November 1935, he organized and led a small guerrilla group against British security forces in the first guerrilla operation of the Palestinian national movement. He died in action with several of his followers, and immediately became a national hero. His martyrdom triggered the Great Rebellion of 1936–39 (see 242ff.), and his example was very much in the minds of PLO leader Yasser Arafat and Arafat's colleagues three decades later.

The Countryside

Rural Scenes

114 Aerial view of the Mount of Olives, looking toward the Dead Sea.

115 Orchards in Jericho. Many wealthy Palestinians from Jerusalem had winter houses in Jericho.

114

115

116

117

116 Ein Karim, west of Jerusalem.

117 The village and valley of Silwan, just east of the walls of Jerusalem, looking south. In the distance note Government House, the residence of the British high commissioner, on the so-called Hill of Evil Counsel!

118 Abu Ghosh, about fourteen kilometers from Jerusalem, on the road to Jaffa.

119 Beit Sahur seen from Shepherds' Field near Bethlehem, looking east.

118

119

120

120 The hills of Bethlehem. Note the traditional headdress.

121 Water mill on the Auja River near Jaffa.

121

122 Terraced hills seen from Kolonia, a village on the road to Jaffa about eight kilometers west of Jerusalem.

123 The Orthodox monastery of St. George on the Mount of Temptation in the wilderness near Jericho.

122

123

Rural Life through the Lens of
Khalil Raad (See 72, 186)

124 Stonecutters.

125 Fishermen of the Sea of Galilee.

124

125

126

126, 127 Fishermen of the Sea of Galilee.

128 Village carpenters.

129 An extended family in the village of Beit Sahur, near Bethlehem.

127

128

129

130

130 Mother and child.

131 Springtime.

132 Bedouin girls in Jericho.

131

132

133

133 Senior citizens.

134 The peep show.

135 Palestinian "checkers."

134

135

136

136 A village school.

Palestinian Agricultural Production

Contrary to prevailing opinion in the Western world, the Palestinians were responsible for the bulk of agricultural production in the country during the British Mandate. By the end of the Mandate, the total land area under cultivation by Palestinian farmers (excluding citrus) was 5,484,700 dunams (one dunam = one thousand square meters), and the area cultivated by Jewish farmers was 425,450 dunams.[1] With regard to desert cultivation, by 1935 the Palestinians were farming 2,109,234 dunams in the Negev,[2] whereas total Jewish landholdings in the Negev in 1946 did not exceed 21,000 dunams. Thus it was the Palestinians who made the desert bloom! The following figures and percentages for individual crops are taken from an official report of the British Mandatory government of Palestine.[3]

137–140 *Grains:* of 4,367,629 dunams under grain cultivation, the Palestinians owned and cultivated 4,152,438 dunams.

138

139

140

137

141

142

126

143

141 *Bananas:* 60 percent of the area planted with bananas was Palestinian-owned and cultivated.

142 *Vines:* 86 percent of the area planted with vines was Palestinian-owned and cultivated.

143 *Melons:* of 125,979 dunams planted with melons, the Palestinians owned and cultivated 120,304 dunams.

144

144 *Olives:* of 600,133 dunams, 99 percent was Palestinian-owned and cultivated.

145 *Vegetables:* of 279,940 dunams, 239,733 dunams were Palestinian-owned and cultivated.

146 *Tobacco:* the area under tobacco cultivation was restricted by the Mandatory government to avoid overproduction. Virtually all the land under tobacco cultivation was Palestinian-owned.

145

146

129

Livestock

147, 148 The animal wealth of the country was also
largely Palestinian-owned:[4]

	Palestinian-owned	Jewish-owned
Cattle	219,400	28,400
Sheep	224,900	19,100
Goats	314,600	10,800
Camels	33,200	—
Horses	16,900	2,200
Mules	7,300	2,500
Donkeys	105,400	2,300
Pigs	12,100	—
Total:	933,800	65,300

147

148

The Jaffa Orange: The Palestinian Gift to the World

149–157 Today the Jaffa orange is the agricultural product that is most closely associated with Israeli production. Yet Palestinian expertise had already developed the Jaffa orange before Zionist colonization of Palestine got under way. In 1886 the American consul in Jerusalem, Henry Gillman, writing to Assistant Secretary of State J. D. Porter, called attention to the excellent quality of the Jaffa orange and the superior grafting techniques of Palestinian citrus farmers: "I am particular in giving the details of this simple method of propagating this valuable fruit," he reported to Washington, "as I believe it might be adopted with advantage in Florida."[5] It was not until the end of the Mandate that Jewish production managed to catch up with Palestinian production levels. Even then, however, Palestinian citrus production remained slightly ahead, both quantitatively and qualitatively, as this table (in which the areas under cultivation were graded) indicates:[6]

	Class 1	Class 2	Class 3	Total Dunams
Palestinian-owned	100,055	17,401	5,502	122,958
Jewish-owned	93,640	13,150	7,562	114,352

149

150

151

152

153

154

155

156

157

158

159

160

158 A general view of Gaza.

159 Gaza street scene.

160 Bethlehem; the second tower from the left is that
     of the Church of the Nativity.

161 Jaffa, from the sea.

162 Jaffa, looking inland.

163 Jaffa, looking out to sea. Until 1936, before the development of the Haifa and Tel Aviv harbors, Jaffa was the main seaport of Palestine.

164 Central Square, Jaffa, soon after the inauguration of the British Mandate. The building with pillars, on the right, is the Grand Serai (see 6, 393).

165 Jaffa, looking toward the new Palestinian residential Nuzhah quarter, ca. 1935. Note the contrast in means of transportation with the previous photograph.

161

162

163

164

165

166

167

140

166 A house interior, Jaffa, ca. 1935.

167 Tiberias, looking south, ca. 1935. The mosque in the foreground, known as the Upper Mosque, was built at the beginning of the eighteenth century.

168 Tiberias, looking north toward Mount Hermon, ca. 1935.

169 The residence of the Taji family, Wadi Hunayn, near Ramleh, ca. 1934.

170 A general view of Jenin.

168

169

170

71–173 Views of Nazareth.

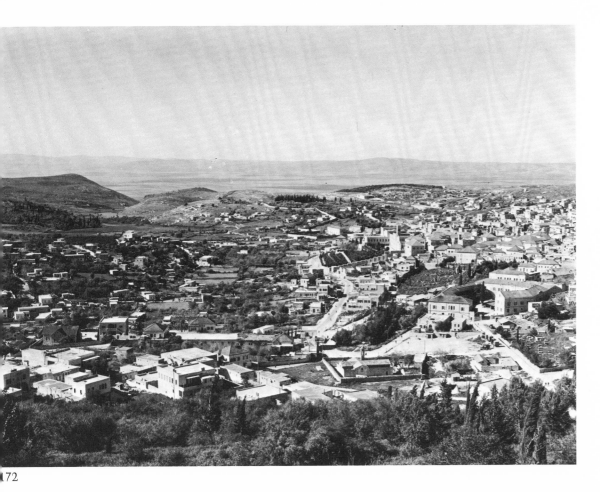

172

173

174

174 The fountain at Bab al-Silsilah (Gate of the Chain), built during the reign of Suleiman the Magnificent (1520–66), the Old City of Jerusalem.

175 Taxi stand, Damascus Gate, Jerusalem, ca. 1928. Damascus Gate and the Old City walls (see 176) were also built by Suleiman the Magnificent.

176 Looking west at the Old City of Jerusalem from the Palestine Archaeological Museum, ca. 1937. In the middle ground is Bab al-Zahirah (Herod's Gate). The building nearest right is the al-Rashidiyyah Secondary School for Boys.

175

176

177 Looking northeast at a Palestinian residential
quarter just outside Bab al-Zahirah, Jerusalem.

178 The Old City of Jerusalem under snow, looking
toward the Mount of Olives.

177

178

Religious Monuments and Sites

179 The inner courtyard of the Jazzar Mosque at Acre, built in 1781 by Ahmad al-Jazzar, who in 1799 checked the advance of Napoleon through Palestine with the help of a British naval squadron commanded by Sir Sydney Smith. Revered relics of the prophet Muhammad (hairs from his beard) are housed in this mosque.

180 The tomb of Leah with embroidered drapery, in the Mosque of Abraham, Hebron. The Arabic lettering reads: "This is the tomb of our Lady Leah; blessings of Allah be upon her, wife of the prophet Jacob; peace be upon him." (See 28–29, 38, 183, 207–208)

179

180

181

181 The mosque at Beersheba; its architecture is late Ottoman.

182 The Grand Mosque in Gaza, originally a twelfth century A.D. structure.

183 The Muslim shrine and mosque at the site of the tomb of Nabi Daoud (the prophet David), outside the Old City walls, Jerusalem. (See 28 et al.)

184 The Via Dolorosa, Fifth Station of the Cross, in the Muslim Quarter of the Old City, Jerusalem.

182

183

184

185

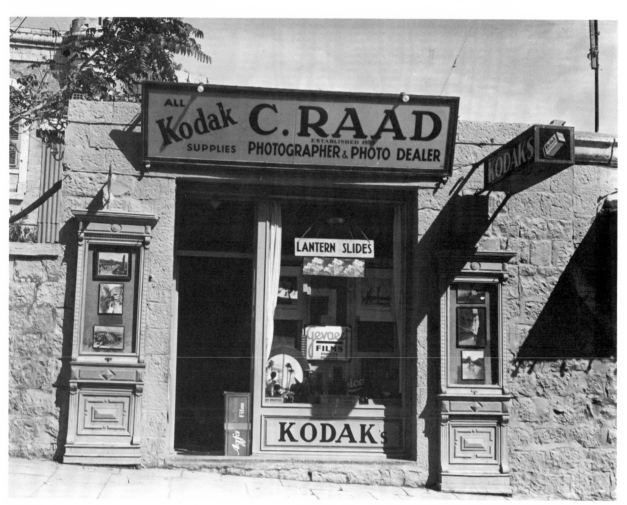

186

Craftsmen, Tradesmen, and Artisans

187

188

185 A vegetable stand.

186 Khalil Raad's shop, Jaffa Gate, Jerusalem (see 72, 124–136).

187, 188 Jewelers in the Old City of Jerusalem (187) and the Old City of Acre (188).

189–191 The ancient crafts of the weaver (189) and the potter.

192 Quiltmakers.

189

190

191

192

193

193 Suq al-Attarin (the Spice Market).

194

Aspects of Urban and Religious Life

194 A Christian wedding, Haifa, 1930. The bride-groom is Hanna Asfour, a Catholic Palestinian lawyer (see 250, 270); the bride, Emily Abu Fadil.

195 A Muslim wedding, Wadi Hunayn, near Ramleh, 1935. The bridegroom is Nazif al-Khairi, a district officer; the bride, Samiyah Taji.

195

198

199

196 Mayor of Jerusalem Raghib al-Nashashibi (see 100, 242, 352), standing center, gives a tea party at his home in honor of Shaikh Abd al-Hayy al-Kittani (seated to his right), a Moroccan religious leader and scholar, on the latter's visit to Jerusalem in 1930. The other guests are Palestinian notables and dignitaries. The child is the visitor's son. Seated nearest right is Awni Abd al-Hadi (see 100, 291).

197 The Arab Medical Conference (YMCA, Jerusalem, 1933), attended by physicians from various Arab countries. The British high commissioner, Sir Arthur Wauchope (center, front row), opened the conference (see 243b–243c). To his right are Ali Ibrahim Pasha, then the leading Egyptian surgeon; and Raghib al-Nashashibi, mayor of Jerusalem. Fourth right, front row, is Izzat Tannous (see 63).

198 Ali al-Kassar (front center), an Egyptian actor, visits friends in Jerusalem, 1934. Seated first right is Fawzi al-Ghosein from Ramleh, a graduate in law from Cambridge University, England.

199 Palestinian musicians and singers at the Palestine Broadcasting Station, Jerusalem, 1936.

200

201

202

203

200 Masquerading as Indian maharajas and maharanis at the home of Mr. and Mrs. Alfred Roch, Jaffa, 1924. The host (a Palestinian Catholic notable) is first left, second row; standing center, third row, is the hostess (see 100, 242, 291).

201 The Holy Sepulcher, Maundy Thursday, 5 April 1934. Presiding is the Christian Orthodox patriarch. Precariously seated on the scaffolding is Wasif Jawhariyyah (wearing a fez). He was the owner of a valuable collection of photographs from which many items for this album have been selected (see 71).

202 Haj Amin al-Husseini (see 82), mufti of Jerusalem, flanked by Christian religious dignitaries, ca. 1930. To his right are the Greek patriarch and the Coptic bishop, respectively, and to his left, the Armenian patriarch and the Abyssinian abbot. This photograph illustrates the unusual degree of harmony that existed between the Christians and Muslims of Palestine.

203 Orthodox Jews and others in European dress returning from a visit to the Wailing Wall, mid-1930s (see 55, 90).

204

205

206

204 Samaritan Jews (in the foreground) celebrating
their Passover, Nablus, early 1930s. The Samaritans were a tiny Jewish sect numbering less than
two hundred, most of whom lived in Nablus.
They used Arabic for everyday speech, but a dia-
lect of Aramaic in their liturgy. From the Old
Testament they accepted only the Pentateuch.
Note their turbans.

205 A conference of Palestinian Christian Orthodox
priests, Ramallah, September 1932.

206 Ahmad al-Sharif al-Senussi (holding a staff) visits
the Haram al-Sharif (see 1) in Jerusalem, ca.
1923. He was a leader of the Libyan Senussi *tar-
iqah*, a religious brotherhood.

207

208

207, 208 Al-Nabi Musa ("the Prophet Moses") was the
name given to one of the most important annual
religious festivals celebrated by Palestinian Muslims; it entailed a procession on foot or on horse-
back from Jerusalem to the traditional burial site
of Moses, near Jericho (see 28–29, 38, 180, 183).
Vast crowds from different parts of Palestine
gathered for the occasion. These photographs
show Jaffa Gate (207) and St. Stephen's Gate
(208), in Jerusalem, during the festival. The
mufti of Jerusalem (seen mounted in 208) led the
procession. The custom of celebrating this festival went back to the thirteenth century. Al-Nabi
Musa is an excellent example of how deeply imbued Muslim Palestinians were with the Jewish
heritage.

Aspects of Educational and Cultural Life

Schools for Palestinians under the Mandate could be divided into three kinds: public (government), private (both Palestinian Christian and Muslim), and foreign (Christian). By 1947 some 130,000 Palestinian students out of a Palestinian population of 1,238,000 were attending elementary and secondary schools. This number comprised approximately 85 percent of school-aged boys from the towns and 63 percent from the villages. For girls the figures were 60 percent and 7.5 percent, respectively. The public system was the largest of the three, but was hampered by insufficient funds. Government expenditure on education averaged only 4.5 to 5 percent of the total budget throughout the Mandate. (The largest single item of expenditure was "security," occasioned by the government's suppression of Palestinian resistance to its pro-Zionist policies.) Because of insufficient funds, the proportion of admissions to applications at government schools, even during the last decade of the Mandate, averaged less than 64 percent, where schools were available; in at least half of the ca. eight hundred villages they were not. However, the desire for education in the villages was so great that the villagers eagerly contributed not only village lands as sites for schools, but also free labor and cash for their construction. Voluntary cash contributions from villagers for educational and other village social services alone rose from £P 18,285 in 1941 (the Palestinian pound was equivalent to the pound sterling), to £P 86,961 in 1942, to £P 288,464 in 1945.

"The Least Worthy of You Are the Least Learned"

209 Staff and alumni of the Dusturiyyah (Constitutional) School, ca. 1919 (see 61); a typical private school. The founder, Khalil Sakakini, is seated first left. Behind him is George Khamis, a gifted Christian Orthodox teacher of English grammar, who mended the English syntax of hundreds of Palestinian students.

210 The Jerusalem Girls' College, ca. 1920; founded by a British Anglican mission. The staff are in the last two rows. The majority of the student body was Palestinian, both Christian and Muslim.

209

210

الهيئة التدريسية
للمدرسة الثانوية الأميرية بيافا
٢٨ حزيران ٢٢

211

فرقة
كرة القدم الأولى للمدرسة الثانوية
يافا - ١٩٢٣

212

164

213

214

215

214 Carpentry class, 1924. The inscription over the
door reads, "The least worthy of you are the least
learned."

215 Inter-school Field Day, Jaffa, 1924.

اثر من آثار المغفوله تأييد الأهالي شيخ عمر زنبيس رحمه الله

المنظر العمومي لأساتذة وتلامذة مدرسة العرفان الوطنية الإسلامية بنابلس
المصور عيسى صوابيني من يافا ١٣٤١ سنة ١٩٢٤

216

الصف الخصوصي المنتهي في مدرسة النجاح الوطنية بنابلس   ذكرى أنهاء الدراسة في المدرسة ١٣٤٢ سنة   المصور عيسى صوابيني في يافا

217

216 Students, including Wolf Cubs, and staff of the Irfan (Knowledge) School, Nablus, 1924; a private school founded in 1922.

217 The staff and graduating class of the Najah (Success) School, Nablus, 1924; a private school founded in 1918. It became the nucleus of the present Najah University on the West Bank.

المنظر العمومي لأساتذة وتلامذة مدرسة النجاح الوطنية

بنابلس سنة ١٣٤٣
١٩٢٤

المصور عيسى صواييني في يافا

218

218 The student body, including Scout troops, and staff of the Najah School, Nablus, 1924.

219 The student body and staff of the private Wataniyyah (National) School, Jerusalem, 1925. Seated center is the indefatigable founder and headmaster, Khalil Sakakini (see 61, 209).

220 The staff of the private Salahiyyah School (so called after Saladin), Nablus, 1926. Seated first right is an Egyptian member of the staff — an example of the cultural contact between Palestine and neighboring Arab countries (see 233, 235).

219

220

221

222

The All-Palestine Boy Scout Jamboree

221 Bir Salim, near Ramleh, 1926. Seated center, third row, is Humphrey Bowman, British director of the Department of Education.

Ladies in a Kindergarten

222 "Sample" of the kindergarten class at a German Protestant mission school, Schmidt Girls' College, Jerusalem, 1926 (see 241). The young ladies in the picture are *all* from the same family, the Tajis of Wadi Hunayn, near Ramleh. Note the symmetrical arrangement of the toys.

The YMMA

223 The founding members of the YMMA — the Young Men's Muslim Association — modeled on the YMCA; Acre, 1928.

The Acre Sports Club

224 Members of the Sports Club, Acre, 1928. Third right, second row, is Ahmad Shukairi (see 69, 105), later to become chairman of the PLO (Palestine Liberation Organization).

Graduates of British Universities

225 Palestinian students at British universities celebrating the wedding of one of their members, Izz al-Din al-Shawwa, London, 1928. Seated left to right, first row, are Khulusi al-Khairi from Ramleh (Public Administration, London School of Economics); unidentified woman; Izz al-Din al-Shawwa from Gaza (Agriculture, Cambridge University); the bride; Wasfi Anabtawi from Nablus (Geography, Cambridge University); Mrs. W. Anabtawi. Second row: Wasif Kamal from Nablus (Law, London University); Muhammad Hadid and Taha Abd al-Baqi (both Iraqi colleagues); Anis al-Bibi from Jaffa (Economics, Cambridge University). Last row: Diya al-Din al-Khatib from Jerusalem (History, London University); Nazif al-Khairi from Ramleh (Public Administration, London University); Khalil al-Budeiri from Jerusalem (Ophtalmology, London University).

223

224

225

226

The Pinnacle of Palestinian Education: The Arab College

226 Staff and students of the Arab College at its old premises, Bab al-Zahirah (Herod's Gate), Jerusalem, 1930. As the highest Palestinian educational institution in the country, the Arab College was distinguished for its stringent admissions requirements and for its equal emphasis on both the Islamic-Arab heritage and the Western classical and liberal traditions (see 240). By the end of the Mandate, it had evolved into a university-level college; its seniors qualified for London University's B.A. degree, and many of its graduates were sent on scholarships to the United Kingdom. The staff (seated, second row) included Ahmad Tuqan, second left, from Nablus (Physics, Cambridge University), who later became chief of the Royal Cabinet and prime minister of Jordan; the principal of the college, Ahmad Samih al-Khalidi, center, from Jerusalem (Psychology, American University of Beirut), author of several volumes on pedagogy that became standard textbooks in several Arab countries, and translator into Arabic of works by M. Montessori and the German psychologist W. Stekel; and Muhammad Haj Mir, third right (History, Tübingen University).

227

227 Staff and students of the Arab College at its new premises on Jabal al-Mukabbir, "the Mount of the Glorifier," south of Jerusalem, 1938. (This was the site from which the caliph Omar, on his way to Jerusalem to accept its capitulation from the Byzantines in A.D. 637, first caught a glimpse of the city, only to fall on his knees and glorify God.) Note the blazers of the students (standing) with the college badge, a falcon clutching an ink-horn. Standing first left, last row, is Jabra Jabra (later a graduate in English literature from Cambridge University), poet and author of many works of literary criticism and fiction including the novel *Hunters in a Narrow Street* (London: Heineman, 1960), as well as translator into Arabic of several plays by Shakespeare. Seated among the faculty (fourth left) is Wasfi Arafat from Nablus (Mathematics, London University). Next to him (fifth left) is Izhak Musa Husseini from Jerusalem (School of Oriental Studies, London University), author of several works on Islamic and Arab history in addition to *The Diaries of a Hen*, an Orwellian work of fiction satirizing the plight of the Palestinians under the Mandate.

228

229

. . . And Its Base: The Village School

228, 229 At the other end of the spectrum were the
village schools. The two schools pictured here
are typical of some 420 village schools that existed in Palestine by the end of the Mandate. In
photograph 229, the boys are going through their
morning drill before entering class. Note their
satchels on the ground.

230

231

Collège des Frères

230 The staff and graduating class of the Collège des Frères in Jerusalem, 1934. This secondary school was founded by the Franciscan Order in 1875.

St. George's School Revisited

231 The boarding students, 1932.

175

232

233

234

232 The Scout troop, 1935. (See 62–64)

Moroccan Students in Nablus

233 The staff and graduating class of the Najah (Success) School, Nablus, 1932. Seated in the front row, right to left, are Akram Zu'aiter, journalist, orator, and activist from Nablus, who became foreign minister of Jordan in 1966; Muhammad Adnani, a poet from Jenin; Qadri Tuqan, mathematician and author of a history of Arab science, from Nablus; Shaikh Abd al-Hamid al-Sa'ih, later minister for religious affairs in Jordan; and the headmaster Jalal Zurayq, poet and mathematician. In the last row (left to right) the second, ninth, and tenth students are Moroccan; their attendance at the school is another example of the cultural interaction between Palestine and the Arab world. (See 220, 235)

Terra Sancta

234 Terra Sancta College for Boys in Jerusalem, 1932; also founded by the Franciscan Order (see 230).

Palestinian Teachers in Iraq

235 Young Palestinian teachers pursuing higher studies in Iraq, 1934. Seated center is Akram Zu'aiter, then lecturer at the Teachers' Training College, Baghdad. This photograph illustrates again the cultural interaction between Palestine and the Arab world. (See 220, 233)

235

236, 237 Students (236) and school band (237) of the
National Christian Orthodox School, Jaffa, 1938.
The school was founded in 1921 by the Christian
Orthodox Welfare Society.

236

Band – National Sec. Orth. school 15/6/38.

238

239

Rowing on the Cam

238 Abdurrahman Bushnaq (graduate of the Arab College in Jerusalem), stroke of Jesus College rowing crew (second left), on the River Cam, Cambridge University, where he read English literature, 1935. (See 226, in which Bushnaq is the sixth person left, third row.) His publications include a translation into Arabic of *The Splendid Spur* by Sir Arthur Quiller-Couch, editor of the *Oxford Book of English Verse*.

The Arab College in the 1940s

239 Keeping fit.

240 Brushing up their Latin. The lecturer, George Hourani, graduated from Oxford University and wrote several books including *Arab Seafaring in the Indian Ocean in Ancient and Early Medieval Times* (Princeton University Press, 1951) and *Islamic Rationalism* (Oxford: Clarendon Press, 1971). He later taught philosophy at the State University of New York at Buffalo. Note the college's emblem. (See 226–227)

Schmidt Girls' College Again

241 The older ladies at the school, Jerusalem, 1947 (see 222).

240

241

From Homer's "Odyssey" to "Practical Chemistry"

241a–241p A mélange of sixteen books by Palestinians, published before 1946. The titles of the first eight, in English, are

241a *Practical Chemistry*, by Salim Katul;

241b *Introduction to the Eastern Question*, by Ruhi al-Khalidi;

241c *Readings in Philology and Literature*, by Khalil al-Sakakini;

241d *My Vision*, by Arif al-Arif;

241e *Modern Science and Us*, by Is'af al-Nashashibi;

241f *Medieval European Portraits*, by Nicola Ziyadeh;

241g *Lectures in Mercantile Law*, by Francis Khayyat;

241h *Translation of "The Odyssey" of Homer*, by Anbarah Salam al-Khalidi.

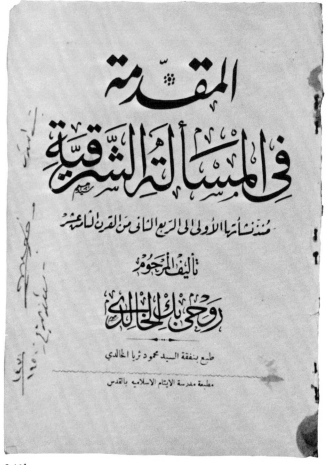

241b

241a

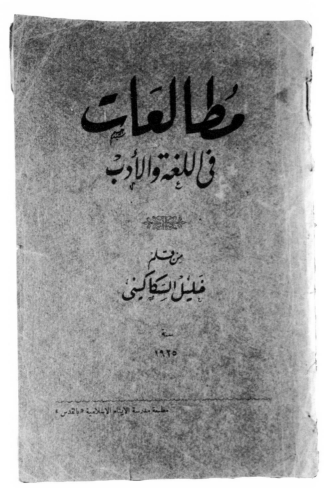

مُطالَعات
في اللغة والأدب

من قلم
خليل السكاكيني

سنة
١٩٢٥

مطبعة مدرسة الأيتام الإسلامية بالقدس

241c

رُؤيَاي

تأليف

عارف العارف

حقوق الطبع والنقل والترجمة محفوظة للمؤلف

مطبعة الآباء الفرنسيسيين في بيت المقدس
١٣٦٢ ه‍ ــ ١٩٤٣ م

241d

كلمة موجزة
في
سير العلم وسيرتنا معه
بقلم
إسعاف النشاشيبي

طبع في مطبعة دار الأيتام السورية. في بيت المقدس سنة ١٩١٦

241e

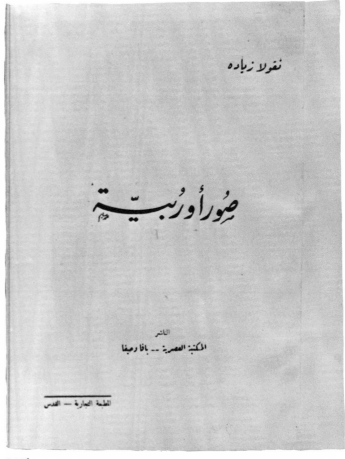

نقولا زياده

صُوَر أوروبية

الناشر
المكتبة العصرية ــ يافا وحيفا

المطبعة التجارية ــ القدس

241f

محاضرات
في
القانون التجاري

فرنسيس خياط
القاضي في محكمة الاستئناف العليا بفلسطين

طبع في مطبعة دير الروم بالقدس سنة ١٩٢٤

241g

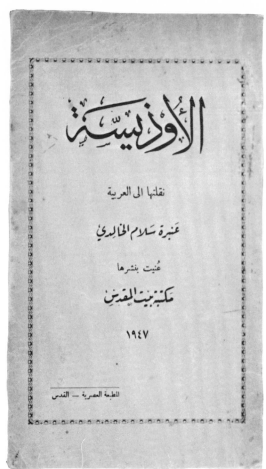

الأوذيسية

نقلتها الى العربية

عنبرة سلام الخالدي

عُنيت بنشرها

مكتبة بيت المقدس

١٩٤٧

للطبعة العصرية ــ القدس

241h

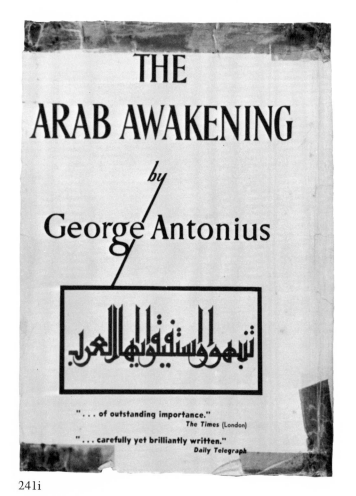

THE
ARAB AWAKENING

by

George Antonius

تنبه واستيقظ ايها العرب

"... of outstanding importance."
The Times (London)

"... carefully yet brilliantly written."
Daily Telegraph

241i

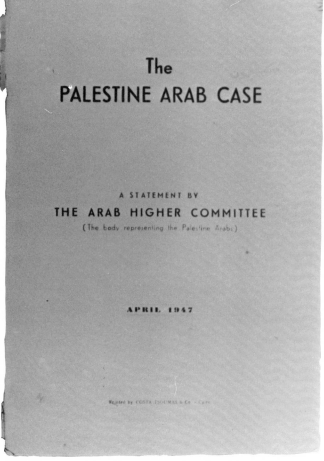

The
PALESTINE ARAB CASE

A STATEMENT BY

THE ARAB HIGHER COMMITTEE
(The body representing the Palestine Arabs)

APRIL 1947

Printed by COSTA TSOUMAS & Co - Cairo

241j

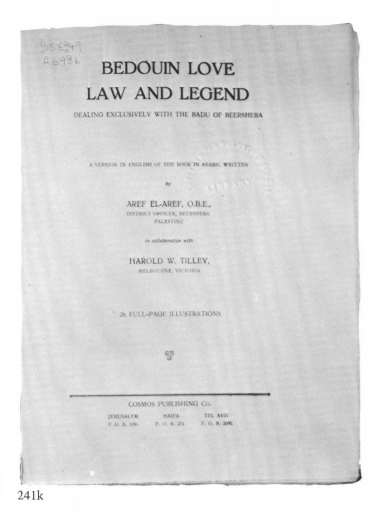

BEDOUIN LOVE
LAW AND LEGEND

DEALING EXCLUSIVELY WITH THE BADU OF BEERSHEBA

A VERSION IN ENGLISH OF THE BOOK IN ARABIC WRITTEN

by

AREF EL-AREF, O.B.E.,
DISTRICT OFFICER, BEERSHEBA
PALESTINE

in collaboration with

HAROLD W. TILLEY,
MELBOURNE, VICTORIA

26 FULL-PAGE ILLUSTRATIONS

COSMOS PUBLISHING Co.

JERUSALEM   HAIFA   TEL AVIV
P. O. B. 1091   P. O. B. 274   P. O. B. 2092

241k

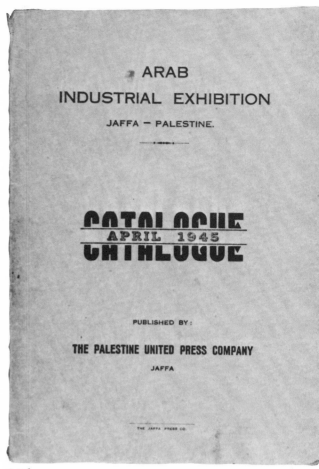

ARAB
INDUSTRIAL EXHIBITION

JAFFA — PALESTINE.

CATALOGUE
APRIL 1945

PUBLISHED BY :

THE PALESTINE UNITED PRESS COMPANY

JAFFA

THE JAFFA PRESS CO.

241l

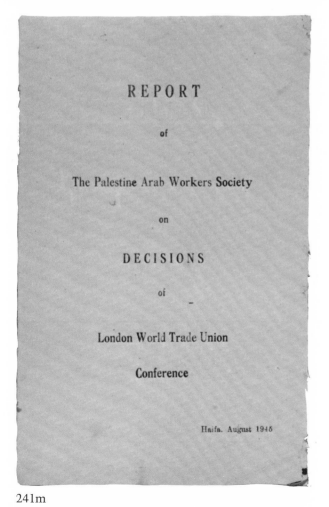

REPORT

of

The Palestine Arab Workers Society

on

DECISIONS

of

London World Trade Union

Conference

Haifa, August 1945

241m

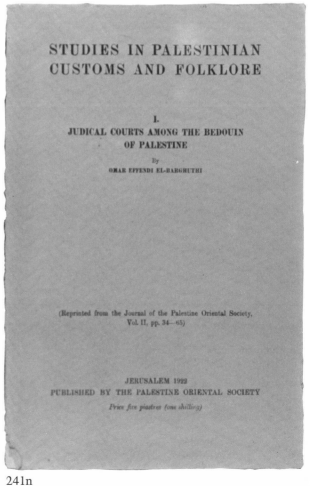

STUDIES IN PALESTINIAN
CUSTOMS AND FOLKLORE

I.
JUDICAL COURTS AMONG THE BEDOUIN
OF PALESTINE

By

OMAR EFFENDI EL-BARGHUTHI

(Reprinted from the Journal of the Palestine Oriental Society,
Vol. II, pp. 34—65)

JERUSALEM 1922
PUBLISHED BY THE PALESTINE ORIENTAL SOCIETY

Price five piastres (one shilling)

241n

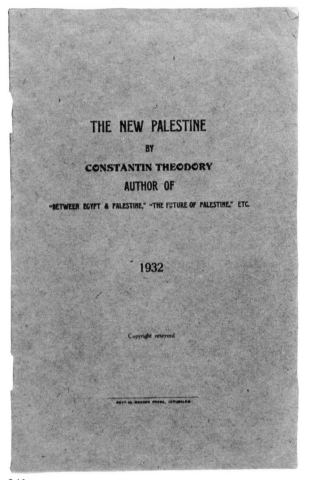

241o

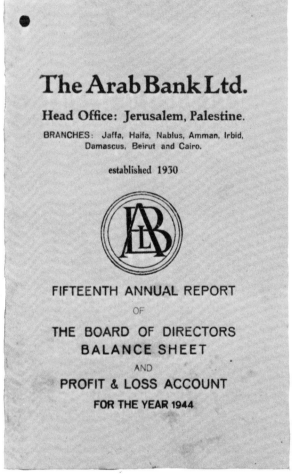

241p

PART III

THE GREAT REBELLION

1936–1939

INTRODUCTION

BY early May 1936 the Palestinians were in open rebellion. National Committees, which would become the organizational base of the rebels, had been established in April in all the Palestinian towns and larger villages. Before the end of the month, all five Palestinian political parties had united to form the Arab Higher Committee under the chairmanship of Haj Amin al-Husseini. The pressure on Haj Amin to act now intensified. On May 8 he summoned a conference in Jerusalem of all the National Committees. Raising the cry of "No taxation without representation," the conference called for civil disobedience and a general strike to protest British pro-Zionist policies.

THE FIRST PHASE

The rebellion endured for three years and fell into three phases. The first phase lasted from May 1936 to July 1937, with the general strike continuing for the first six months of it, from May until October 1936. The strike was strictly observed and brought commercial and economic activity in the Palestinian sector to a standstill. Unrest spread to the countryside, where villagers took up arms and engaged the British security and military forces in open guerrilla warfare.

The British rushed in reinforcements and demolished parts of the Old City of Jaffa as a punitive measure. Some volunteers from the Arab countries came to the aid of the Palestinian rebels, but the brunt of the fighting was borne by the Palestinians themselves. The British intensified their military operations, simultaneously sending a commission of inquiry under Lord Peel to ascertain the causes of the rebellion. The heads of the neighboring Arab states then appealed to the Arab Higher Committee to call off the general strike and appear before the Peel Commission. On October 11, the Arab Higher Committee acceded to their request. There was a short lull in the rebellion between November 1936 and January 1937 while the commission toured the country. But tension subsequently mounted again until it exploded in unprecedented violence in July 1937.

THE SECOND PHASE

The second phase of the rebellion lasted from July 1937 until the fall of 1938. What triggered the new escalation of violence was the publication in July 1937 of the Peel Commission's report, which unhesitatingly declared that "the underlying causes of the disturbances" were two: the desire of the Palestinians for independence, and their "hatred and fear of the establishment of the Jewish national home." The report then proceeded to recommend the partition of the country into a Jewish state, a Palestinian state to be incorporated by Transjordan, and enclaves reserved for the Mandatory.

The Palestinians were outraged by these recommendations. They could not accept the legitimization of a Zionist political title in Palestine. Hundreds of Palestinian villages would fall within the Jewish state, and hundreds of thousands of Palestinians would become a subject minority in it. The Jewish state would acquire about 33 percent of the total area of the country (including the fertile regions of Galilee, all Palestinian-owned, and the coastal plain from the Lebanese border to Jaffa, owned equally by the two communities) at a time when Jewish ownership did not exceed 5.6 percent of Palestine.

The Palestinians feared the confiscation of their land inside the Jewish state through the application of the guidelines governing the activities of the Jewish National Fund. They resented the incorporation of the proposed Palestinian state into Transjordan. Above all they were horrified at the commission's recommendation that they be forcibly transferred, if necessary, out of the Jewish state. Even the commission itself sounded sheepish in its summing up of the report when it hypocritically argued, "Considering what the possibility of finding a refuge in Palestine means to many thousands of suffering Jews, is the loss occasioned by partition, great as it would be, more than Arab generosity can bear?"

The British responded to the escalating Palestinian resistance by determining to break its backbone. Seizing the opportunity afforded by the assassination, in September 1937, of a British senior administrator in Nazareth by Palestinians, they promptly outlawed the Arab Higher Committee in addition to all Palestinian political parties and organizations. They arrested scores of Palestinian leaders and exiled five principal ones to the Seychelles Islands in the Indian Ocean. They threw thousands of Palestinians into special "detention camps"; among those detained were professionals, civil servants, clergymen, students, and farmers. In combat they used their air force, tanks, and heavy artillery against the rebels. Military tribunals passed summary sentences, including death by hanging, for the possession of arms. Collective punishment was imposed on towns and villages by blowing up entire residential quarters, closing schools, levying fines in kind or cash, and billeting troops at the expense of the residents.

At the same time, the British built up Jewish military strength. In cooperation with the Jewish Agency's secret army, the Haganah, they organized, trained, and armed a special force called the Jewish Settlement Police (JSP), which by early 1939 was 14,000 strong. In June 1938 they created an Anglo-Jewish unit called the Special Night Squads (SNS) for "special operations" against Palestinian villages. It was during this second phase of the rebellion that the new tactics of throwing grenades and planting time bombs in crowded marketplaces were introduced into the Zionist-Palestinian conflict by the Irgun Zvai Leumi (National Military Organization), the military branch of the right-wing Zionist Revisionist Party.

In 1938 alone the number of Palestinians killed in action by the British was conservatively estimated at not less than one thousand, while 54 Palestinians were executed by hanging, and 2,463 Palestinians were detained. The Palestinian population at the time did not exceed one million.

In spite of all these measures the Palestinian rebellion continued unabated during 1938, and several areas of the country, including the Old City of Jerusalem, fell under rebel control. Palestinian resistance elicited strong expressions of support and solidarity from the neighboring Arab countries. In September 1937 a popular pan-Arab congress, held in Bludan, Syria, endorsed Palestinian opposition to partition. Palestinian demands were again endorsed in October 1938 by the Arab Parliamentarians' Congress and the Arab Women's Congress, both held in Cairo.

THE THIRD PHASE

The third phase of the rebellion extended from the fall of 1938 until the summer of 1939. The British seemed to be moving on two tracks. As early as April 1938, they had dispatched another commission of inquiry, under the chairmanship of Sir John Woodhead, ostensibly to study the technical aspects of the implementation of partition. The Woodhead Commission's report was published in November 1938, and its general conclusion was that partition was not practicable. Nevertheless, the British planned an all-out offensive to crush the rebellion. They brought in massive new reinforcements and transferred the administration of the country to military commanders. The ensuing engagements were the severest so far. Fifty-five Palestinians were executed by hanging, at least twelve hundred Palestinians were killed in action by the British, more than twice as many Palestinians were detained as in the previous year (1938), and five times as many rifles were seized from Palestinians in a drive to achieve their total disarmament.

With the publication of the Woodhead report, the British government also announced its intention to hold a general conference in London to be attended both by Zionist and Palestinian leaders and by representatives of the neighboring Arab countries. However, the British shortsightedly vetoed the participation in the conference of paramount Palestinian leader Haj Amin al-Husseini, chairman of the still-outlawed Arab Higher Committee. After escaping arrest in September 1937, Haj Amin had been directing the rebellion from his exile in Lebanon. The London Conference lasted from 7 February to 27 March 1939 without reaching a settlement satisfactory to the Zionists and Palestinians.

In May the British government published a new White Paper in which it undertook to implement, irrespective of Palestinian and Zionist objections, the policy enunciated: Britain's obligations to the Jewish national home had been substantially fulfilled; indefinite mass Jewish immigration to and land acquisition in Palestine would contradict Britain's obligations to the Palestinians; within the next five years, 75,000 more Jews would be allowed into the country, after which Jewish immigration would be subject to "Arab acquiescence"; land transfers would be permitted in certain areas, but restricted and prohibited in others, to protect the Palestinians from landlessness; and an independent unitary state would be established after ten years conditional on favorable Palestinian-Jewish relations.

Many Palestinians were positively impressed with the White Paper, but could not accept it because of the ambiguity of the phrase "Arab acquiescence" in relation to continuing future Jewish immigration, and the conditional nature of the promised independent unitary state. The Zionists accused the British of "appeasing" the Arabs and consulting their strategic interests in the area due to the deterioration of the international situation. The 1939 White Paper marked the beginning of the end of the Anglo-Zionist entente ushered in by the Balfour Declaration in 1917.

CHRONOLOGY

1936 April 16: Two Palestinians living near Petah Tikva shot dead by Zionist assailants.

April 20–30: National Committees established in all Palestinian towns and large villages.

April 21: Leaders of all five Palestinian political parties call for general strike.

April 25: Leaders of Palestinian political parties constituted as Arab Higher Committee under chairmanship of Haj Amin al-Husseini.

May 8: Conference of all National Committees, meeting in Jerusalem, calls for no taxation without representation. Great Rebellion begins.

May 11: British bring military reinforcements from Malta and Egypt into Palestine.

May 18: British appoint Royal Commission to investigate causes of rebellion.

June: British demolish parts of Old City of Jaffa as punitive measure.

June 30: All Palestinian members of civil service and judiciary submit joint memorandum to high commissioner protesting British pro-Zionist policies.

August 25: Guerrilla leader Fawzi al-Qawukji enters Palestine at head of 150 volunteers from Arab countries to aid rebellion against British.

August 30: Arab Higher Committee announces continuation of general strike, but expresses readiness to accept mediation by Arab heads of state.

September 22: Additional British reinforcements arrive in Palestine; extensive military operations initiated against Palestinian rebellion.

October 11: Arab Higher Committee accepts appeals by kings of Saudi Arabia and Iraq, and emir of Transjordan, to call off general strike.

November 11: Royal Commission, under chairmanship of Lord Peel, arrives in Palestine.

1937 January 18: Royal (Peel) Commission leaves Palestine.

July 7: Publication of Royal (Peel) Commission's report recommending partition of Palestine into Jewish state, Arab state (to be incorporated into Transjordan), and British Mandatory enclaves, as well as forcible transfer, if necessary, of Palestinian population out of Jewish state.

July 23: Arab Higher Committee rejects Royal Commission's partition proposal and demands independent unitary Palestinian state "with protection of all legitimate Jewish and other minority rights and the safeguarding of reasonable British interests." Rebellion intensifies.

August: World Zionist Congress in Zürich decides to ascertain "the precise terms . . . for the proposed establishment of a Jewish state."

September: Arab National Congress, held in Bludan, Syria, and attended by 450 delegates from Arab countries, rejects Royal Commission's partition proposal, and demands termination of Mandate, cessation of Zionist immigration into Palestine, and prohibition of transfer of Arab lands to Zionist ownership.

September 5: Bomb thrown by Irgunists at bus in Jerusalem kills one Palestinian and injures another.*

---

* Among the reasons for attributing the bombings against Palestinian civilians between 1937 and 1939 to the Irgun, rather than the Haganah or the Stern Gang, are these: (1) Such actions were very much in keeping with Revisionist thinking, (2) Revisionists were arrested by the British in connection with some of the incidents, (3) the Revisionists were totally opposed to partition, (4) the Haganah was cooperating with the British authorities during this period and therefore was unlikely to be engaged in such actions, (5) the Stern Gang had not yet been founded, and (6) the Irgun was openly calling for the colonization of both Palestine and Transjordan by force.

October 1: British dissolve Arab Higher Committee and all Palestinian political organizations. Five Palestinian leaders deported to Seychelles Islands in Indian Ocean; Haj Amin al-Husseini escapes to Lebanon.

November 11: British establish military courts throughout Palestine to counter escalating rebellion.

Bomb thrown in Jerusalem by Irgunists kills one Palestinian and wounds three.

November 14: Three Palestinians killed in Irgunist attack on bus in Jerusalem.

1938 January 4: British decide to send technical commission of inquiry, under chairmanship of Sir John Woodhead, to study feasibility of partition as recommended by Royal Commission.

March 1: Sir Harold MacMichael succeeds General Sir Arthur Wauchope as high commissioner.

April 17: Two bombs thrown by Irgunists into café in Haifa kill one Palestinian and one passing Jew, and wound six Palestinians.

April 27: Technical commission of inquiry (Partition Commission) arrives in Palestine.

June: British officer Orde Wingate organizes Special Night Squads (SNS), composed of British and Haganah personnel, for operations against Palestinian villages.

July 4: Bomb thrown by Irgunists at bus in Jerusalem kills four Palestinians and wounds six.

July 6: Twelve Palestinians die from bomb thrown by Irgunists into Haifa melon market.

Bomb thrown by Irgunists into Haifa marketplace kills 18 Palestinians and 2 Jews.

July 7: Bomb thrown by Irgunists into Jerusalem vegetable market kills one Palestinian and wounds five.

July 8: Bomb planted by Irgunists explodes in Jerusalem bus station, killing 4 Palestinians and wounding 27.

July 15: Bomb planted by Irgunists in Jerusalem (Old City) vegetable market kills 11 Palestinians and injures 28.

July 17: Three Palestinians found murdered in Tel Aviv; police arrest five Zionist Revisionists.

July 25: Bomb planted by Irgunists in Haifa vegetable market kills 45 Palestinians and wounds 45.

July 30: Bomb thrown by Palestinians at bus in Haifa kills one Jew and wounds ten.

August 3: Partition (Woodhead) Commission departs Palestine.

August 4: Land mine planted by Palestinians blows up truck near Ramat Hakovesh; six Jews killed and eight injured.

August 18: Bomb thrown by Palestinians along Jaffa–Tel Aviv border kills one Jew and injures four.

August 26: Bomb planted by Irgunists in Jaffa vegetable market kills 23 Palestinians and wounds 30.

October: Arab Parliamentarians' Congress on Palestine, held in Cairo, endorses three demands of Palestinian national movement as stated by Arab National Congress at Bludan, Syria, in September 1937 (see above).

Arab Women's Congress, meeting in Cairo, endorses demands of Palestinian national movement.

October 18: British military commanders take over administrative control from district commissioners throughout country to increase pressure on Palestinian rebellion; new reinforcements brought in from England.

October 19: British troops recapture Old City of Jerusalem from Palestinian rebels.

November 9: Partition (Woodhead) Commission publishes report stating impracticality of Royal Commission's partition proposal. British call for general conference on Palestine to be held in London and attended by Arab, Palestinian, and Zionist representatives.

December: Palestinian leaders previously deported to Seychelles Islands released, but denied return to Palestine.

1939 January 20: Bomb planted by Palestinians in Haifa workshop kills one Jew and injures five.

February 7: London Conference opens at St. James's Palace.

February 26: Bomb planted by Irgunists in Haifa marketplace kills 24 Palestinians and injures 37.

Bomb planted by Irgunists in Jerusalem vegetable market kills four Palestinians and wounds five.

Bomb thrown by Palestinians at truck in Haifa kills two Jews.

March 27: London Conference ends with no agreement reached.

May 17: Malcolm MacDonald, colonial secretary of state, issues White Paper of 1939 embodying British solution to Palestine problem:

conditional independence for unitary Palestinian state after interval of ten years, admission of 15,000 Jewish immigrants annually into Palestine for five years, and protection of Palestinian land rights against Zionist acquisition.

May 22–23: British House of Commons votes 268 to 179 to approve White Paper of 1939.

June 2: Bomb planted by Irgunists in Jerusalem bus station kills 5 Palestinians and wounds 19.

June 3: Bomb planted by Irgunists in Jerusalem kills 9 Palestinians and injures 40.

June 19: Bomb planted by Irgunists in Haifa marketplace kills 9 Palestinians and wounds 24.

June 29: Six Irgunist attacks on buses traveling roads near Tel Aviv cause death of 11 Palestinians.

July 3: Bomb thrown by Irgunists into Haifa café kills one Palestinian and wounds 35.

August 1: Irgun calls for conquest of Palestine by force.

September 1: Outbreak of World War II.

October: Stern Gang, formed under Avraham Stern by dissident Irgunists, in protest against 1939 White Paper policy, calls for alliance with Axis powers in war against British.

242

The Arab Higher Committee

The Arab Higher Committee, comprising representatives of all Palestinian parties, was formed on 25 April 1936. One of its first acts was to call for a general strike and civil disobedience "to continue . . . until . . . the formation of a national government responsible to a representative assembly, the prevention of the transfer of Arab lands to the Jews, and the stoppage of Jewish immigration."

242 Front row, left to right: Raghib al-Nashashibi, former mayor of Jerusalem and leader of the Defense Party (see 100, 196, 352); Haj Amin al-Husseini, mufti of Jerusalem and president of the

Arab Higher Committee; Ahmad Hilmi, chairman of the Ummah (People's) Bank and affiliated with the Istiqlal (Independence) Party (see 102, 105); Abd al-Latif Salah, chairman of the National Bloc Party; and Alfred Roch, Catholic notable from Jaffa affiliated with the Palestine Arab Party (see 100, 200, 291). Second row, left to right: Jamal al-Husseini, chairman of the Palestine Arab Party; Dr. Hussein al-Khalidi, mayor of Jerusalem and secretary of the Reform Party; Ya'qub al-Ghusayn, president of the Arab Youth Congress; and Fuad Saba, Protestant notable and secretary of the Arab Higher Committee. (See 268–269, 291, 344)

243

243 Residents of Abu Ghosh, a village west of Jerusalem (see 118), taking the oath of allegiance to the Arab Higher Committee, April 1936.

"No Taxation without Representation" — May 1936

243a Typical of political posters appearing at the beginning of the general strike.

243a

الانتداب بعد ١٩ سنة

After 19 Years of British Mandate

اللنبي في القدس سنة ١٩١٧

Allenby in Jerusalem – 1917

واكهوب في القدس سنة ١٩٣٦

Wauchope in Jerusalem – 1936

243b

Jemal Pasha to Sir Wauchope

« Many many thanks . . . The Arabs have now forgotten my tyranny and bless my memory . »

روح جمال باشا تناجي السير واكهوب :-

« انا قبلك سجنت وابعدت وقتلت وشنقت وهدمت واكني في النهاية فشلت ...

فاشكرك شكرا جزيلا لانك جعلت العرب ينسون مظالمي ويترحمون على عهدي ... »

243c

After Nineteen Years

243b, 243c These caricatures appeared in the Jaffa daily *Filastin* in April 1936. The uniformed figure with plumed hat is General Sir Arthur Wauchope, the British high commissioner at the time. In 243b, Wauchope abandons his cane (and top hat!) for a sword in order to attack the Old City on a tank; his action is contrasted with Allenby's attempt, upon entering Jerusalem in 1917, to allay Palestinian fears with the words "lest any of you should be alarmed" (see 16). Jemal Pasha (in 243c), the Turkish governor general of Syria-Palestine during World War I, was remembered for his brutal suppression of nationalist sentiments (see 8–9). The caricatures illustrate the depths of Palestinian disillusionment with British pro-Zionist policies.

244

M32 9029

245

Searches

244–246 Steel-helmeted British troops search a Palestinian in Jaffa (244) . . . and in Jerusalem (245) look under a fez just in case! A South African police dog (246) comes to the aid of the British. This last photograph and details are taken from the *Illustrated London News*, June 1936.

246

THE POLICE DOG USED IN AN ATTEMPT TO TRACK ONE OF THE ARABS WHO ATTACKED CAPTAIN SIGRIST : ONE OF TWO TRAINED ANIMALS IMPORTED FROM SOUTH AFRICA.

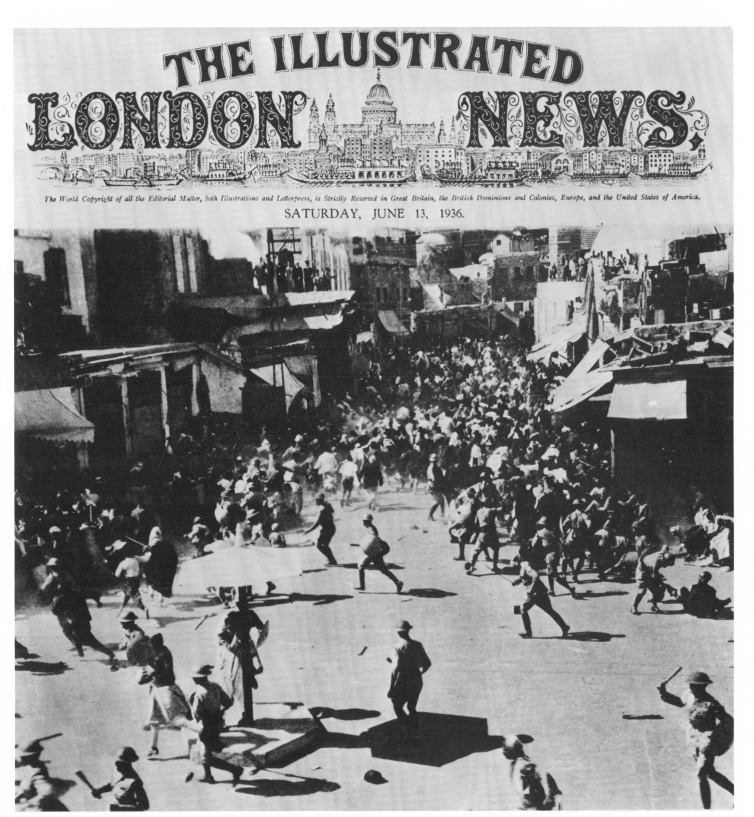

The World Copyright of all the Editorial Matter, both Illustrations and Letterpress, is Strictly Reserved in Great Britain, the British Dominions and Colonies, Europe, and the United States of America.

SATURDAY, JUNE 13, 1936.

247

Demonstrations

247 British riot police clash with Palestinian demonstrators and make front-page news in London; Central Square, Jaffa, 1936.

Detention Camps

Thousands of Palestinians from all walks of life were held in detention camps during this period. For the numbers of Palestinians interned from 1937 to 1939, see 282.

248 Inmates in a detention camp while away the time.

249 A Christian Orthodox priest is held alongside Muslim religious dignitaries in a detention camp. Cross-legged on the floor is Michel Mitri, the Christian Orthodox head of the Jaffa Labour Union, also detained.

250 First left is Hanna Asfour, Greek Catholic lawyer and legal adviser to the Arab Labour Society in Haifa (see 194, 270). Traditional dress was worn by urban detainees as a gesture of defiance.

250

249

MEMORANDUM

SUBMITTED BY

ARAB SENIOR GOVERNMENT

OFFICIALS

ON JUNE 30TH, 1936,

TO HIS EXCELLENCY

THE HIGH COMMISSIONER FOR PALESTINE

ON THE PRESENT SITUATION
IN THE COUNTRY.

250a

Revolt of the Civil Servants

250a–250g *"Authority implies justice all round, and when justice is denied. . . ."* All Palestinian senior officials, without exception, signed a joint memorandum submitted on 30 June 1936 to the British high commissioner; the memorandum supported Palestinian national demands as formulated by the Arab Higher Committee (see 242). The list of signatories and their titles indicate both the range of Palestinian administrative and professional talent already in public service in the mid-1930s, and the extent to which the Palestinian national movement had crystallized by then.

the Colonies. In view, however, of the seriousness of the situation and the difficult position in which we find ourselves, we would request Your Excellency to cable the substance of this memorandum to the Secretary of State and favour us with a reply at your earliest possible convenience.

We have the honour to be,

Your Excellency's Obedient Servants,

SIGNATORIES:-

JUDICIAL DEPARTMENT.

1. Mustafa Bey El Khalidi C. B. E. Puisne Judge, Supreme Court, Jerusalem.
2. Francis Khayat — Puisne Judge, Supreme Court, Jerusalem.
3. Majid Bey Abdul Hadi—Puisne Judge, Suprem Court, Jerusalem.
4. Abdel Aziz Shaker El Daoudi—Judge, District Court, Jaffa.
5. Izzat Nammar — Judge, District Court, Haifa.
6. Ali Hasna — Judge, District Court, Jerusalem.
7. Muhammad Yusuf El Khalidi — Judge, District Court, Nablus.
8. Muhammad Said Bey Tuqan — Judge, District Court, Nablus.
9. Muhammad Baradey — Senior Magistrate, Jerusalem.
10. Antone Atalla — Senior Magistrate, Jerusalem.
11. Rafiq Abu Ghazaleh — Senior Magistrate, Haifa.
12. Sheikh Omar Souan — Magistrate, Ramle.
13. Taher Afghani — Magistrate, Hebron and Beersheba.
14. Sheikh Ismail Kamal — Magistrate, Tulkarm.
15. Nasib Munib Bey Tuqan — Magistrate, Jenin.
16. Musa Nammar — Magistrate, Jaffa.
17. Sheikh Muhiddin El-Mallah — Magistrate, Nablus.
18. Amin Nasr — Magistrate, Bethlehem and Ramallah.
19. Jamil Habibi — Magistrate, Haifa.
20. Iskandar George Khoury — Magistrate, Jerusalem.
21. Jamal ed-Din Dabbagh — Magistrate, Majdal.
22. Khalil Shehadeh — Magistrate, Jaffa.
23. Zaki Tamimi — Magistrate, Haifa.
24. Ali Zein el-Abdin — Magistrate, Jerusalem.
25. Aziz Jarjura — Magistrate, Safad, Tiberias and Khalsa.
26. Saleh Abdel Ghani — Magistrate, Gaza.
27. Hanania Hanania — Magistrate, Jerusalem.

250b

8

28. Sam'an Daoud — Magistrate, Acre.
29. Elias Khoury — Magistrate, Nazareth and Beisan.

CHIEF SECRETARY'S OFFICE.

30. Ruhi Bey Abdul Hadi O.B.E. — Assistant Secretary, Jerusalem.
31. I. F. Kaabani — Acting Chief Interpreter (Arabic), Jerusalem.

LEGAL DEPARTMENT.

32. Musa El Alami O.B.E. — Acting Solicitor General, Jerusalem.
33. Fauzi Ghussein — Acting Government Advocate, Jerusalem.
34. Omar Wa'ari — Junior Government Advocate, Jerusalem.

PERSONAL STAFF.

35. Ihsan Hashem — Private Secretary, Jerusalem.

TREASURY.

36. M. F. Abcarius, O.B.E. — Senior Assistant Treasurer, Jerusalem.
37. J. Gress — Senior Assistant Treasurer, Jerusalem.
38. A. K. Saba — Assistant Treasurer, Jerusalem.
39. S. Jouzy — Assistant Treasurer, Jerusalem.
40. Rajai Husseini — Assistant Treasurer, Jerusalem.

DISTRICT ADMINISTRATION.

41. Nasuhi Bey Beydun, M.B.E. — Administrative Officer, Jerusalem.
42. M. Nasir — Administrative Officer, Ramleh.
43. Rafiq Bey Beydun, M.B.E. — Administrative Officer, Haifa.
44. Abdul Razzak Kleibo, M.B.E. — Administrative Officer, Gaza.
45. A. J. Mantoura — Administrative Officer, Jerusalem.
46. N. Saba — Administrative Officer, Jerusalem.
47. D. Farradji — Administrative Officer, Ramallah.
48. A. Kardus, M.B.E. — Administrative Officer, Hebron.
49. N. Bawarshi, M.B.E. — Administrative Officer, Acre.
50. W. Isawi — Administrative Officer, Nazareth.
51. B. Nasir, M.B.E. — Administrative Officer, Gaza.
52. Aref Al-Aref, M.B.E. — Administrative Officer, Beersheba.
53. H. Husseini, M.B.E. — Administrative Officer, Tulkarm.
54. H. Boulos — Administrative Officer, Tiberias.
55. T. Yazdi — Administrative Officer, Nablus.
56. J. A. R. Tukan — Administrative Officer, Ramle.
57. A. Nashashibi, — Administrative Officer, Jaffa.

250c

9

58. N. Khairy — Administrative Officer, Jerusalem.
59. I. Shawa — Administrative Officer, Jenin.
60. K. Khairy — Administrative Officer, Jerusalem.
61. F. Sa'ad — Administrative Officer, Nazareth.
62. A. Khayr — Administrative Officer, Beisan.
63. R. Shawa — Administrative Officer, Haifa.

HEALTH DEPARTMENT.

64. D. Boulos, M.B.E.—Assistant Senior Medical Officer, Jerusalem.
65. Z. Haddad, M.B.E.—Assistant Senior Medical Officer, Jaffa.
66. M.K. Mishalany—Medical Officer, Jaffa.
67. J. Tucktuck — Medical Officer, Nazareth.
68. F. K. Abla — Medical Officer, Jerusalem.
69. A. Abdul Al, O.B.E. Medical Officer, Hebron.
70. K. Eid — Medical Officer, Nablus.
71. Farid Haddad — Inspector of Pharmacies, Jerusalem.
72. F. I. Haddad — Medical Officer, Haifa.
73. Y. Hajjar, M.B.E. — Medical Officer, Jerusalem.
74. I. Hawrani — Medical Officer, Ramallah.
75. H. S. Khalidi — Medical Officer, Jaffa.
76. Taher El Khatib — Medical Officer, Jenin.
77. A. A. Shihadeh — Medical Officer, Acre.
78. F. Shubeitah — Medical Officer, Jaffa.
79. E. Sikkarieh — Medical Officer, Safad.
80. K. M. Abu Ghazaleh — Medical Officer, Gaza.
81. Naif A. Hamzeh — Medical Officer, Haifa.
82. M. A. Shukair — Medical Officer, Jerusalem.
83. A. I. Haddad — Medical Officer, Ramle.
84. A. M. Shihadeh — Medical Officer, Jaffa.
85. I. Itayim — Medical Officer, Gaza.
86. S. Saleem, O.B.E. — Medical Officer, Beersheba.
87. W. Itayim — Assistant Analyst, Jerusalem.
88. S. Shihab — Medical Officer, Hebron.
89. M. S. Dabbagh — Assistant Bacteriologist, Jerusalem.
90. A.K. Khartabil—Medical Officer, Tulkarm.
91. A.A. Sururi—Medical Officer, Nablus.
92. S. Bishara — Medical Officer, Nablus.
93. S.N. Barnick—Medical Officer, Tiberias.
94. I. Ali Alamud Din—Medical Officer, Jerusalem.
95. Rafat Amin Faris—Medical Officer, Jerusalem.
96. A. Bishara—Medical Officer, Jerusalem.

250d

97. Said Dajani— Medical Officer, Haifa.
98. S. M. Katkhuda —Medical Officer, Jerusalem.

DEPARTMENT OF CUSTOMS, EXCISE & TRADE.

99. F.A. Mansour—Surveyor, Jerusalem.
100. R. Carmi—Surveyor, Haifa.
101. J. Ayoub—Surveyor, Haifa.

COMMISSIONER FOR LANDS & SURVEYS.
A. LAND REGISTRATION.

102. Said 'Ala ud Din—Land Officer, Jerusalem.
103. Y.J. Atallah—Land Officer, Jerusalem.
104. A. Nseibeh—Land Officer, Jerusalem.

B. LANDS & SURVEYS.

105. T. Khalidi—Assistant Settlement Officer, Field.
106. A. Salem—Assistant Settlement Officer, Tulkarm.
107. Ihsan Es-Said—Assistant Settlement Officer, Jaffa.

PALESTINE RAILWAYS.

108. N.G. Tibshirani—Assistant District Traffic Superintendent, Haifa.

OFFICE OF THE REGISTRAR OF CO-OPERATIVE SOCIETIES.

109. R. Khalidi—Inspector, Jerusalem.

DEPARTMENT OF ANTIQUITIES.

110. N. Makhouly—Inspector, Acre.
111. D.C. Baramki—Inspector, Jerusalem.
112. J. Baramki—Assistant Keeper, Jerusalem.
113. S.A.S. Husseini—Inspector, Jerusalem.

BROADCASTING STATION.

114. Ibrahim Tuqan—Sub-Director, Arabic Programme, Jerusalem.

DEPARTMENT OF AGRICULTURE & FORESTS.

115. Ahmad Khairy—Veterinary Officer, Tiberias.
116. F. Taha—Agriculture Lecturer, Tulkarm.

250e

11

EDUCATION DEPARTMENT.

117. Ahmad Samih al Khalidi, M.B.E.—Principal, Government Arab College, Jerusalem.
118. Jibrail Katul, M.B.E.—Senior Inspector (Arab Schools), Jerusalem.
119. Habib Khuri, M.B.E.—Vice Principal Government Arab College, Jerusalem.
120. Sheikh Husameddin Jarallah, M.B.E. Headquarters Inspector.
121. Sharif Sbuh—District Inspector, Jerusalem.
122. Jamil Zananiri — District Inspector, Haifa.
123. Manasseh M. Hannush—Headquarters Inspector, Jerusalem.
124. Mustafa Dabbagh—District Inspector, Haifa.
125. Ahmad Khalifa—District Inspector, Tulkarm.
126. Khalil Sakakini—Assistant Inspector, Jerusalem.
127. Wasfi Anabtawi—Lecturer, Government Arab College, Jerusalem.
128. Sharif Nashashibi—Headmaster, Acre.
129. George Khamis—Lecturer, Government Arab College, Jerusalem.
130. Salim Katul—Lecturer Government Arab College, Jerusalem.
131. Anis Sidawi—Headmaster, Haifa.
132. Muhamad Haj Mir—Headmaster, Jerusalem.
133. Ishaq Musa al-Husaini—Lecturer, Jerusalem.

PUBLIC WORKS DEPARTMENT.

134. A. Toukan—Assistant Engineer, Jerusalem.

DEPARTMENT OF MIGRATION.

135. N. Nashashibi—Inspector of Migration, Jerusalem.

OFFICE OF STATISTICS.

136. F.S. Khoury—Junior Statistician, Jerusalem.
137. S.W. Dajani—Junior Statistician, Jerusalem.

N.B. The following officials, who at time of signing were absent, have cabled their solidarity in confirming the contents of the Memorandum :—

JUDICIAL DEPARTMENT.

1. Salim Shehadeh George — Senior Magistrate, Jaffa.

12

DISTRICT ADMINISTRATION.

2. N. Anabtawi — District Officer, Jaffa.

LANDS AND SURVEYS.

3. Mitri Hanna — Land Officer, Jerusalem.
4. T. Nasr — Assistant Settlement Officer, Field.
5. J. K. Awad — Assistant Settlement Officer, Field.

EDUCATION DEPARTMENT.

6. Afif 'At'ut — District Inspector, Nablus.
7. Rafiq Tamimi — Headmaster, Jaffa.
8. Nureddin Abbasi — Assistant District Inspector, Nablus.
9. Alaeddin Halawa — Headmaster, Tulkarm.

DEPARTMENS OF AGRICULTURE AND FORESTS.

10. Abdel Fattah Sabassi — Veterinary Officer, Gaza.
11. Muhammad Sidky — Veterinary Officer, Nablus.
12. Jamal Hassan Hamad — Agriculture Officer, Jerusalem.
13. R. G. Khawam — Science Master, Tulkarm.

BROADCASTING STATION.

14. Yahia Lababidi — Sub-Director, Arabic Music, Jerusalem.

BEYT-UL-MAKDES PRESS. JERUSALEM

250f

250g

252

When All Else Fails

251 Villagers welcoming mounted guerrillas, summer 1936.

Sabotage

252 A train derailed by guerrillas, summer 1936.

253

254

Guerrilla Leaders, Summer 1936

253 Abd al-Qadir al-Husseini (center) with aides. Abd al-Qadir, a graduate of the American University of Cairo in chemistry and the son of Musa Kazim Pasha al-Husseini (see 78, 84–86, 100–101, 104, 111–112), was guerrilla commander for the Jerusalem district. He died in action in the same area during the 1948 War (see 396, 409–411).

254 Second right is Abd al-Halim al-Julani, guerrilla commander for the Hebron district. The banner is the Palestinian national flag.

255 Hamad Zawata, guerrilla commander for the Nablus district.

255

Palestine and Oil

256 The oil pipeline to Haifa from Iraq sabotaged by guerrillas, summer 1936. This was probably one of the earliest instances of the impingement of the Palestine problem on the flow of oil to the West. In the foreground are members of the Jewish Settlement Police (JSP), who were organized and armed by the British to fight the Palestinians. The JSP remained in existence until the end of the Mandate. (See 279–280)

The Punishment of Jaffa, June 1936

As a punitive measure against the Palestinians, the British military blew up large sectors of the Old City of Jaffa, ostensibly for "town-planning purposes." To his credit the chief justice of Palestine, Michael F. J. McDonnell, chastised the government for throwing "dust in people's eyes by professing to be inspired with aesthetic or quasi-philanthropic motives. . . ." His Honor was subsequently relieved of his post. (See 283)

257 The British cordon off the Old City of Jaffa before the demolition starts.

258–261 Scenes of destruction.

256

257

210

258

259

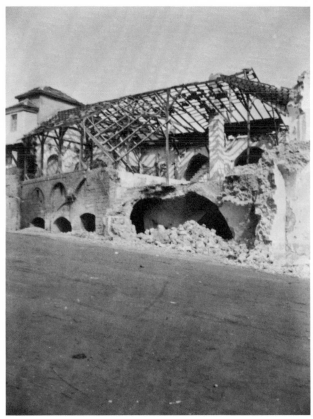

261

260

262

262 But a dead cat is saved!

Volunteers from Arab Countries

263 On 25 August 1936 Fawzi al-Qawukji (third right) infiltrated into Palestine at the head of some 150 volunteers from neighboring Arab countries. Lebanese by birth, Qawukji was something of a Garibaldi figure in Arab popular perception. In 1920 he fought the French invasion of Syria, and later organized resistance to the French Mandatory authorities there. Exiled from Syria by the French, he served as military adviser to Saudi Arabia before going to Iraq, where he held the post of lecturer at the Military Academy in Baghdad. Baghdad was the starting point of his expedition to Palestine, which marks the first "military" intervention (if unofficial) by the Arab countries in support of the Palestinians. Qawukji again led Arab irregular forces in Palestine during the 1948 War (see 403).

264 Qawukji organized the Palestinian guerrillas of central Palestine, and led them through several fierce engagements with British forces in which the latter used planes, tanks, and heavy artillery. Here he is seen taking the salute as a guerrilla column marches past, ca. September 1936. Qawukji and his volunteers left the country on 24 October 1936, after the general strike and rebellion declared by the Arab Higher Committee (see 242) had been temporarily called off at the request of the Arab heads of state. Their request was based on a British promise to send yet another commission of inquiry "to ascertain the underlying causes of the disturbances." Meanwhile, since April 1936 the rebellion had resulted in "upward of 1,000 [Palestinian] rebels killed, mostly in fighting with troops and police." The number of soldiers and police killed was officially put at thirty-seven.[1]

263

264

265

The Peel Commission and Partition

265 The members of the Palestine Royal Commission arrived in Palestine in November 1936. Third left is Lord Peel, chairman of the commission. The commission's report, published in July 1937, found that the underlying causes of the disturbances were the Palestinians' desire for national independence and their fear of the establishment of a Jewish national home. It nevertheless recommended the partition of Palestine into a Jewish state, a Palestinian state to be merged with Transjordan, and British Mandatory enclaves. The Jews, who at the time owned only 5.6 percent of Palestine, were to be *given* 33 percent of the country, from which Peel suggested that the Palestinian inhabitants could be expelled. Palestinians received the report with shock, dismay, and frenzied resistance.

British Reinforcements

266, 267 Royal Air Force armored cars (266) and an
army base just outside the Church of the Nativity in Bethlehem (267). As the Palestinian rebellion exploded again in the wake of the partition
proposal by the Royal Commission, the British
rushed reinforcements to the country.

266

267

Smashing the Palestinian Political Infrastructure

268 On 1 October 1937 the Arab Higher Committee (see 242) was dissolved. Four of its members, Dr. Hussein al-Khalidi and Ahmad Hilmi (seated first and second left) and Ya'qub al-Ghusayn and Fuad Saba (back row), were exiled to the Seychelles Islands in the Indian Ocean, where they are pictured here, 15 December 1938. The chairman, Haj Amin al-Husseini, and others escaped arrest and took refuge in neighboring Arab countries. Exiled with the Seychelles inmates was Rashid al-Haj Ibrahim (seated first right), member of the Istiqlal (Independence) Party from Haifa (see 105). Other measures taken by the British included the dissolution of all political or semipolitical Palestinian organizations and associations, and the arrest of their leaders. (See 289–291)

269 A letter sent by Fuad Saba (see 344) to his children in Jerusalem.

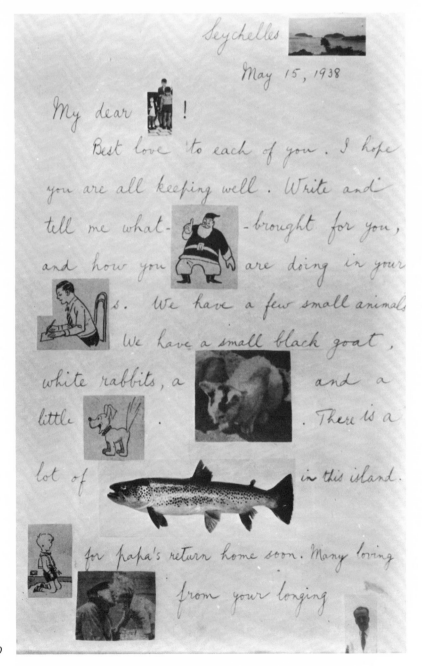

Martial Law

270 On 11 November 1937 military courts were established for the trial of offenses including the
carrying of arms, which was now made punisha-
ble by death. Between 1937 and 1939, the British
executed by hanging 112 Palestinians under the
new law. The robed figure bottom right is Hanna
Asfour, Palestinian legal counsel, who had himself been held in a detention camp (see 194, 250).

270

BRITISH MILITARY COURTS AT WORK IN PALESTINE
Army Officers Who Can Impose the Death Sentence On Those Taking Part in the Campaign of Terrorism

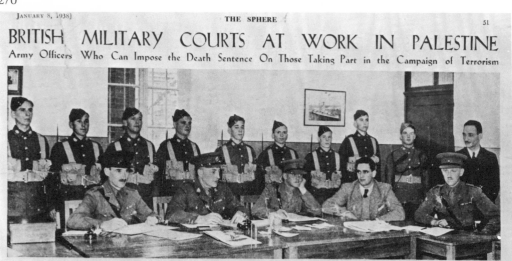

IN SOLEMN SESSION: Major R. H. Welch, D.S.O., of the King's Own Royal Regiment; Major N. E. H. Sim, of the York and Lancaster Regiment; Lieut. D. M. South, of the Hampshire Regiment, and Major J. Y. Calwell, M.V.O., of the Royal Ulster Rifles, sitting in judgment at a military court held in Nazareth to try members of the population believed to have been involved in terrorist activities. The courts were set up on November 10 last following fresh outrages, and the officers may, if necessary, impose the death sentence on persons discharging firearms at troops or civilians and even on those carrying arms. They also deal with a great number of cases of sabotage and intimidation. Ranged behind the judges is a guard provided by the Hampshire Regiment

AN ARAB DEFENDANT GIVES EVIDENCE: The accused protests his innocence while the interpreter listens intently so that he can give a faithful rendering to the judges of the arguments put forward. On the right stands a British guard with fixed bayonet

TELL-TALE EVIDENCE: Major N. E. H. Sim, of the York and Lancaster Regiment, examining with his fellow-judges, bombs and cartridges found in the possession of persons brought before their court for trial

AT THE PRESS TABLE: Reporters, representing Jewish and Arab papers, recording the evidence, and (on right) Hanna Effendi Asfour, of Haifa, a noted advocate, who has been defending many Arabs up for trial

271

272

Aspects of the Resistance, 1938–1939

271 Guerrillas on parade.

272 Note the sole light machine gun (Lewis) on the ground.

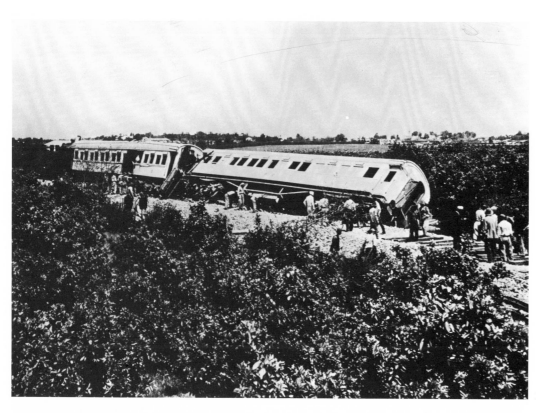

273

274

275

273 More trains derailed.

274 A British armored car and a branch of the British Barclays Bank are targets of attack.

275 One of the most prominent guerrilla leaders of the rebellion, Abd al-Rahim al-Haj Muhammad (center foreground), who died in action against British troops on 28 March 1938.

276 A guerrilla stamp, 1938, showing the Church of the Holy Sepulcher and the Mosque of the Dome of the Rock.

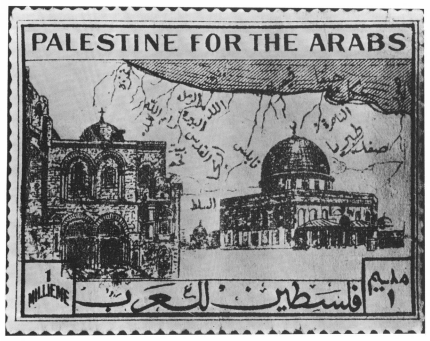

PALESTINE FOR THE ARABS

276

277

277 Collecting contributions for afflicted Palestinian
     families, Jaffa Gate, Jerusalem. Note the Hotel
     Fast on the left.

278

More British Reinforcements

278 Heavy British reinforcements were sent to fight the Palestinians in 1938–39. Some of the leading British officers of World War II held command in Palestine at this time, including Generals J. G. Dill and A. P. Wavell, then Brigadier B. L. Montgomery, and "Bomber" Harris.

Arming One Side and Disarming the Other

279 Fire practice under British supervision at the Jewish settlement of Ein Geb, 1938. The British authorities systematically disarmed the Palestinian population while building up Jewish military strength. By early 1939 the JSP (Jewish Settlement Police; see 256), led by the British, totaled about 14,000.[2] Between 1 September 1936 and 1945, the number of rifles confiscated from Jews was 135 as opposed to 7,617 rifles confiscated from Palestinians.[3] (In 1945 the Jewish population of Palestine was about half the Palestinian population.)

280 The SNS (Special Night Squads) composed of British and Jewish personnel, were organized by the British in 1938–39 to assault Palestinian villages on hit-and-run raids. Here an SNS patrol is led by Orde Wingate, the eccentrically ruthless British officer who created the SNS and first tried out his tactics on the Palestinians before using them in World War II against the Italians (in Ethiopia) and the Japanese (in Burma). In the words of Moshe Dayan, himself trained by Wingate in the SNS: "Every leader of the Israeli Army even today is a disciple of Wingate. . . ."[4]

279

280

224

More Repression

281 British police and army patrols search Palestinians in the Old City of Jerusalem, ca. 1936.

281

282

282 Making collective arrests outside Bab al-Zahirah (Herod's Gate), Jerusalem, September 1938. The British held 816 Palestinians in detention camps in 1937, and 2,463 in 1938. In 1939 they detained 5,679 Palestinians[5] out of a total Palestinian population of ca. one million. This would be roughly equivalent to detaining 1,283,454 Americans, on the basis of the current United States population of ca. 226 million.

283 A favorite British punitive measure was blowing up the houses of "suspects" *and* those of their relatives. Shown here are the ruins of the house of a "suspect" in Jenin, September 1938. (See 257–262)

284 Another favorite punitive measure was the harassment and occupation of Palestinian educational institutions by British troops. In this photograph British troops are encamped on the grounds of the Arab College, Jerusalem, summer 1938 (see 226–227, 239–240).

Since 1967 the Israeli authorities have resorted to similar tactics in the Occupied Territories, citing as justification their earlier use by the British against the Palestinians.

283

284

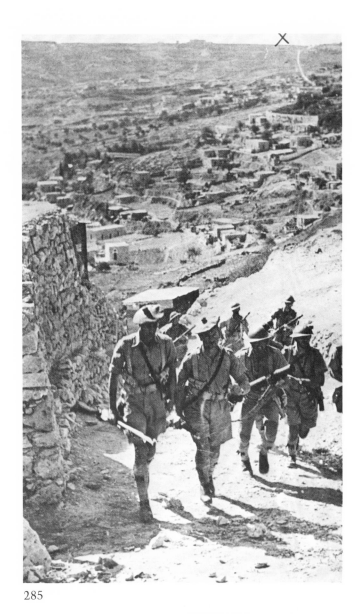

285

The British Reconquest of Palestine, 1938–1939

During this period many parts of Palestine fell under guerrilla control. The British had literally to reconquer these parts of the country from the Palestinians, much as they had conquered the whole country from the Ottomans in World War I. The Old City of Jerusalem, which had fallen under guerrilla control, was recaptured by the British from the Palestinians in October 1938.

285 An advance detachment of British troops moving to the assault just before the recapture of the Old City.

286, 287 Inside the Old City after its recapture.

288 Back in control, the British allow the inhabitants of the Old City to line up for water.

286

287

288

From Repression to Negotiations

By the end of 1939, the Palestinians had been militarily overcome. Conservative estimates of Palestinian casualties for the period 1936–39 are about 5,000 killed and 14,700 wounded out of a total Palestinian population of ca. one million. This would be roughly equivalent to 1,130,000 Americans killed and 3,322,200 wounded, on the basis of the current United States population of ca. 226 million. (For Palestinians detained, see 282.)

289 In December 1938 the Seychelles exiles (see 268–269) were released, but for several years they were not allowed to return to Palestine. Here they are seen at a party held in their honor in Cairo shortly after their release. Seated first left is Abd al-Hamid Shoman, founder of the Arab Bank (see 92).

290 The British government, fearful of the impact of its repressive Palestine policies on British interests throughout the Middle East as World War II approached, and impressed by the intensity of Palestinian resistance, called for a conference to be held in London in February 1939 to discuss the Palestine question. Arab and Jewish delegates were invited. The Arab delegations included representatives from Palestine, Egypt, Yemen, Saudi Arabia, Iraq, and Transjordan. The British vetoed the attendance of the paramount Palestinian leader Haj Amin al-Husseini (see 82, 88, 100, 202), mufti of Jerusalem and chairman of the Arab Higher Committee (see 242). This photograph shows a meeting at the Egyptian Embassy in London attended by the Arab delegates to the London Conference. Seated in the front row, third and fourth right, are Prince (later King) Faisal of Saudi Arabia and Prince (later King) Khalid of Saudi Arabia.

289

290

The London Conference and the White Paper of 1939

291 The London Conference, St. James's Palace, February 1939: a meeting between the British and Arab delegates. The Palestinian delegates are seated in the foreground; from left to right: Fuad Saba (see 242, 268–269, 344), Ya'qub al-Ghusayn (see 242, 268), Musa al-Alami (see 67, 343), Amin Tamimi, Jamal al-Husseini (see 242), Awni Abd al-Hadi (see 100, 196), George Antonius (see 364), and Alfred Roch (see 100, 200, 242). On either side of the Palestinian delegation are the other Arab delegations. Facing the Palestinians are the British, with Sir Neville Chamberlain, prime minister, presiding. To his right is Lord Halifax, secretary of state for foreign affairs, and to his left, Malcolm MacDonald, secretary of state for the colonies.

After the London Conference, the British government issued a White Paper (statement of policy) in which it promised to protect Palestinian land rights in considerable areas of the country against Zionist land acquisition, and to solicit Palestinian "acquiescence" to Zionist mass immigration, but only *after* the admission of 75,000 more Jews during a five-year period. The White Paper also dangled the conditional prospect of an independent unitary state of Palestine, but only *after* a ten-year transitional period.

291

PART IV

FROM THE LONDON CONFERENCE TO THE UN PARTITION RECOMMENDATION

1939–1947

INTRODUCTION

THE period between the end of the Great Rebellion and the events of 1948 unfolded in two phases: the war years (1939–45) and the two years immediately following (1945–47). During the first phase the Palestinians were generally quiescent. Their passivity was due partly to the brutality and thoroughness of the British repression of the rebellion, and partly to the relatively reassuring provisions of the 1939 White Paper on Zionist immigration and land acquisition. Other contributing causes were the economic war boom brought about by an increased level of expenditure on the part of British and Allied forces deployed in the Middle East, and the pronouncements made by British Foreign Secretary Anthony Eden in favor of postwar Arab unity — a cause popular with Palestinian and other Arab nationalists.

THE WAR YEARS

Throughout the war years, and in spite of the 1939 White Paper and Eden's pronouncements, the British continued to outlaw the Arab Higher Committee as well as all other Palestinian political activity. The principal Palestinian leaders remained in hiding, exile, or under arrest; Haj Amin al-Husseini himself escaped jail and worse (the British plotted his assassination in exile) by fleeing in 1941 to the Axis countries, where he spent the remaining war years. In addition, the British continued to hold thousands of Palestinian activists in detention camps, and persevered in their campaign to disarm the Palestinian population. Nevertheless, some eight thousand Palestinians volunteered for service with the British forces in North Africa.

In October 1944 a preparatory conference on Arab unity was held at Alexandria, Egypt. Five months later, in March 1945, the League of Arab States was born. Comprising Egypt, Iraq, Lebanon, Saudi Arabia, Syria, Transjordan, and Yemen, the Arab League pledged itself to safeguard the Arab character of Palestine. As the war drew to a close, many Palestinians looked to the league for help in the coming days.

Anglo-Zionist relations were generally strained during the war as a result of the 1939 White Paper. But the Nazi threat, and especially the North African German expedition against Egypt, muted rising Zionist hostility toward Britain, except in the case of the dissident terrorist group known as the Stern Gang. Some 27,000 Jews from Palestine enlisted in the British forces, and the Jewish industrial base in Palestine was vastly expanded to meet British war requirements.

Both at the beginning of the first phase and throughout the second phase, the 1939 White Paper's policy on immigration was a particular target of Zionist political strategy. In the early war years, the Zionist leadership tried to undermine the White Paper policy by organizing the admission of unauthorized immigrants without reference to the White Paper quota, i.e., instead of using it fully. The British reply was to offer the illegal immigrants alternative accommodation outside Palestine for the duration of the war, but this measure served only to infuriate the Zionists. The Zionists charged that Britain's White Paper policy prevented the rescue of Jews from the barbarities of Nazism; as already noted,[1] however, Zionist prewar immigration strategy itself had not focused on pressuring countries with vast absorptive capacities (e.g., the United States and the British dominions) to admit the maximum number of Jewish refugees from Europe. Moreover, the tragic fact was that the rapid pace of military developments in Europe, and their horrendous consequences for the Jewish communities there, later prevented the Zionist leadership from using even the visas authorized by the White Paper for the five-year period from April 1939 to April 1944. For this reason the British decided in November 1943 to extend the five-year period beyond April 1944 without obtaining Palestinian "acquiescence" as prescribed in the White Paper. In the event, the 75,000 visas permitted by the White Paper were not all used until December 1945.

The most significant indication of the breakdown of the Anglo-Zionist entente occurred during the war years. Early in the war the Zionist leadership in Palestine decided to attempt to activate the American Jewish establishment as a means of mobilizing the United States government on behalf of the Zionist cause. Representing the Jewish Agency, David Ben-Gurion traveled to the United States, where in May 1942 a conference was held at the Biltmore Hotel in New York. Attended by leading American Zionists, the Biltmore Conference called for the establishment of all Palestine as a "Jewish commonwealth" — a euphemism for "Jewish state." This maximalist program constituted a frontal assault on the 1939 White Paper and even on the Balfour Declaration, which had merely envisioned a Jewish national home *in* Palestine. As the tide of war receded from Egypt and North Africa, but before Hitler had been defeated, the Irgun and the Stern Gang opened a campaign of terror against the British. Increasing Zionist aggressiveness toward Britain reflected not only increasing American support, but also the steady cumulative shift in the local balance of power — in favor of the Zionists and at Palestinian expense — that had been taking place under British protection over the preceding three decades. If the Zionists were dependent on the British in 1917, this was no longer the case in 1945.

THE ZIONIST CAMPAIGN AGAINST BRITAIN

The second, postwar phase (1945–47) saw the Zionists escalating their confrontation with the British and setting the pace for events that led to London's decision to refer the Palestine problem to the United Nations as a prelude to British abandonment of the Mandate.

The Zionist campaign against the British was waged on three levels: the diplomatic, the military, and the propagandistic. On the diplomatic level, the Zionists found a powerful ally in President Harry Truman soon after his inauguration. Pressuring London first on the immigration issue, Truman repeatedly (in August 1945, June 1946, July 1946, and October 1946) called for the immediate unconditional admission into Palestine of 100,000 Jewish immigrants, thus altogether undermining the 1939 White Paper. Truman's motivation has been attributed to humanitarian considerations, but these should presumably also have been reflected in concurrent and equally urgent efforts to set an example by admitting a proportionate number of Jewish immigrants into the United States.

In August and October 1946, Truman went a step further in his support of Zionism by endorsing a Jewish Agency plan for the partition of Palestine into a Jewish state and a Palestinian state. The plan envisaged the incorporation into the Jewish state of some 60 percent of Palestine at a time when Jewish landownership in the country did not exceed 7 percent. Truman's support for these Zionist territorial ambitions destroyed whatever hopes remained (and they were not plentiful) for negotiated federal or cantonal solutions that the British were proposing at the time.

The Zionist military offensive took the form of terrorist attacks against British personnel and installations. The attacks relied heavily on the use of mines and other explosives, as well as on assassination. It was during this second phase that the car bomb was first introduced, by the Irgun, into urban warfare. For some time the Haganah participated in these attacks, mostly against installations (bridges, harbor and communications facilities, etc.), but decided in the early summer of 1946 to desist for fear of massive British retaliation. The Haganah's military cautiousness toward the British did not, however, prevent it from exploiting the political and psychological advantages resulting from the continued operations of the Irgun and Stern Gang.

Actually, British reaction to the Zionist terror campaign was surprisingly mild, on account of three factors: Britain's war weariness, Zionist support in the United States, and Britain's reluc-

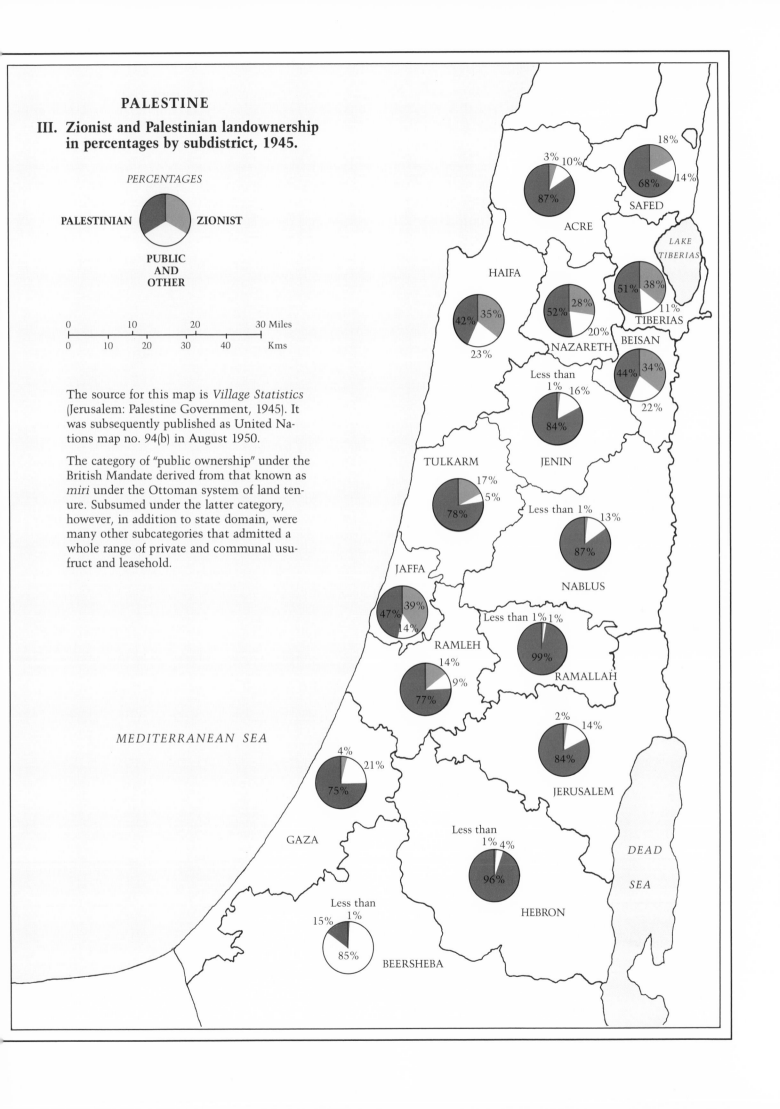

PALESTINE

III. Zionist and Palestinian landownership in percentages by subdistrict, 1945.

PERCENTAGES

PALESTINIAN   ZIONIST

PUBLIC
AND
OTHER

0   10   20   30 Miles

0   10   20   30   40   Kms

The source for this map is *Village Statistics* (Jerusalem: Palestine Government, 1945). It was subsequently published as United Nations map no. 94(b) in August 1950.

The category of "public ownership" under the British Mandate derived from that known as *miri* under the Ottoman system of land tenure. Subsumed under the latter category, however, in addition to state domain, were many other subcategories that admitted a whole range of private and communal usufruct and leasehold.

MEDITERRANEAN SEA

3% 10%
87%
ACRE

18%
68% 14%
SAFED

LAKE
TIBERIAS

HAIFA

42% 35%
23%

52% 28%
20%
NAZARETH

51% 38%
11%
TIBERIAS

44% 34%
22%
BEISAN

Less than
1% 16%
84%
JENIN

TULKARM

17%
78% 5%

Less than 1% 13%
87%
NABLUS

JAFFA

47% 39%
14%
RAMLEH

Less than 1% 1%
99%
RAMALLAH

14%
77% 9%

2% 14%
84%
JERUSALEM

4% 21%
75%
GAZA

Less than
1% 4%
96%
HEBRON

DEAD
SEA

Less than
1%
15%
85%
BEERSHEBA

tance to employ the same measures against a European community that it had resorted to against the Asian Palestinians. Thus, for example, the Arab Higher Committee had been outlawed for eight years, but members of the Jewish Agency were arrested on 29 June 1946 only to be released on November 5 of the same year. The restraint of British countermeasures is perhaps best illustrated by the casualty figures for each side: 169 Britishers killed as compared with 37 Zionist terrorists[2] — probably a unique ratio, in the annals of rebellion, of casualties suffered by security forces in relation to those of the insurgents.

The most effective propaganda tactic used by the Zionist leadership during the postwar phase was the staging of large-scale illegal immigration. Dozens of ships (often unseaworthy) were loaded with Jewish refugees at various European ports and directed by special units of the Haganah toward the shores of Palestine. If they succeeded in evading the British naval patrols, another blow would be struck at the 1939 White Paper; if the British intercepted them, this action could be (and was) presented to the world as callously depriving the wretched remnants of the concentration camps of their only hope of survival.

But the war was at an end, and the survivors of the concentration camps had been removed from their horrible surroundings and put under humane Allied care. There was ample opportunity for countries genuinely concerned on humanitarian grounds to contribute to the alleviation of the survivors' plight by lifting the restrictions on refugee immigration across their own borders. The British government had already reneged in November 1945 on its 1939 White Paper promises by allowing continued Jewish immigration into Palestine (after the exhaustion of the five-year quota) at a monthly rate of fifteen hundred, in spite of the clear absence of Palestinian "acquiescence."

ENTER THE UNITED STATES

The Palestinians and the neighboring Arab countries viewed these developments with growing alarm. Early hopes that American policy would be evenhanded were based on a meeting held at the Suez Canal in February 1945 between President Franklin Roosevelt and King ibn-Saud of Saudi Arabia. At the meeting Roosevelt had assured ibn-Saud that the United States would take no action on the Palestine problem that "would be hostile to the Arabs." Yet within a matter of months President Truman opened his campaign against the 1939 White Paper and soon thereafter declared his sponsorship of Zionist territorial demands. By so doing he began the "dialogue of the deaf" on Palestine that has continued to this day between Washington and the Arab world, and gratuitously launched the Arabs on their path of alienation from the United States.

Although now organized in the Arab League, the Arab countries were far from capable of effective collective action. The league itself was a loose confederal association still very much in its infancy. The dynasties of Saudi Arabia and Egypt were in conflict with those of Iraq and Transjordan. The ruler of Transjordan had dynastic claims in republican Syria and Lebanon. It was not until 1946 that Syria and Lebanon rid themselves of the last French troops left over from the former Mandatory regime. Egypt, Iraq, and Transjordan were all tied to Britain by unequal treaties that considerably circumscribed their power to act in the military, diplomatic, and economic fields. Although Iraq had been producing oil for some time, its oil revenues were minimal as a result of inequitable agreements with Western oil companies. Saudi Arabia was still on the threshold of oil production. Nevertheless, the league countries were all deeply concerned about developments in Palestine. Their publics instinctively sympathized with the Palestinian cause and demanded government action in its support.

Throughout the postwar phase, the cornerstone of Arab League strategy was to pressure Britain to adhere to the 1939 White Paper. This pressure was exerted mainly through quiet diplomacy and negotiations. Some Arab countries (as well as Arab public opinion in general) demanded economic sanctions against Western oil interests in retaliation for American pro-Zionist policies; but no official Arab consensus was ever reached on the subject. Inside Palestine, Arab League strategy was to avoid involvement in the fighting between the Zionists and the British, to encourage conciliation between Palestinian factions, and

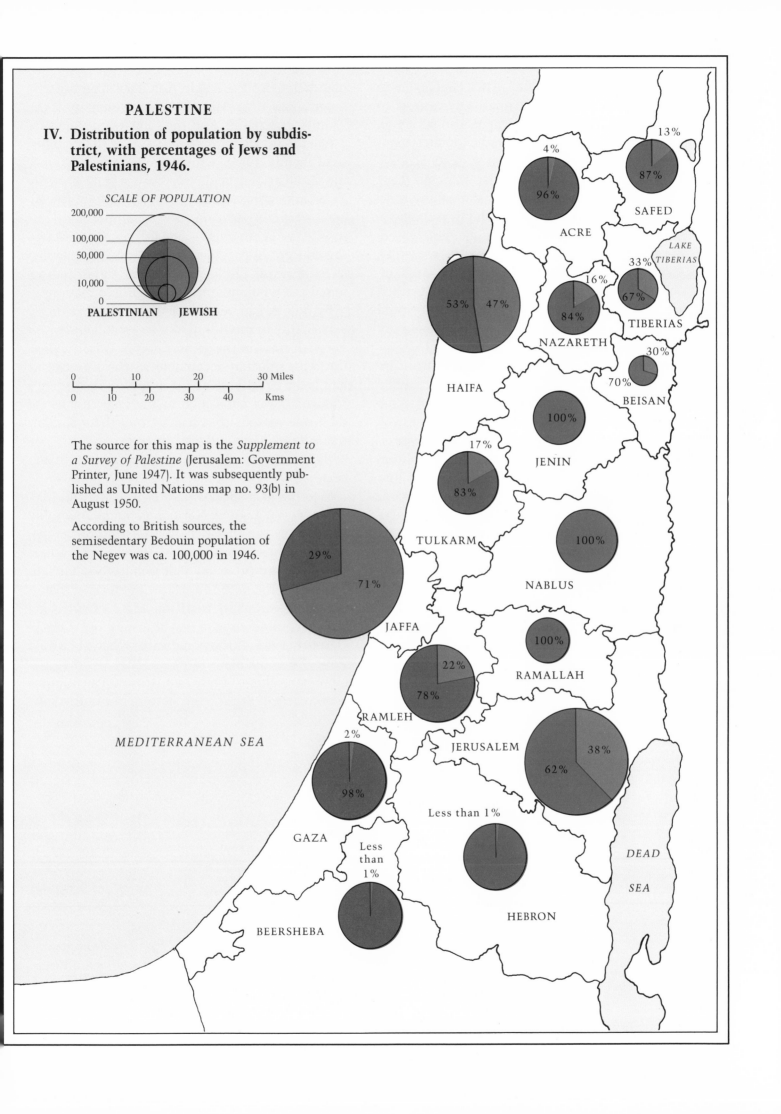

PALESTINE

IV. Distribution of population by subdistrict, with percentages of Jews and Palestinians, 1946.

SCALE OF POPULATION

200,000
100,000
50,000

10,000

0

PALESTINIAN   **JEWISH**

0   10   20   30 Miles

0   10   20   30   40   Kms

The source for this map is the *Supplement to a Survey of Palestine* (Jerusalem: Government Printer, June 1947). It was subsequently published as United Nations map no. 93(b) in August 1950.

According to British sources, the semisedentary Bedouin population of the Negev was ca. 100,000 in 1946.

MEDITERRANEAN SEA

13%
87%
SAFED

4%
96%
ACRE

LAKE TIBERIAS

33%
67%
TIBERIAS

16%
84%
NAZARETH

53%   47%
HAIFA

30%
70%
BEISAN

100%
JENIN

17%
83%
TULKARM

100%
NABLUS

29%
71%
JAFFA

22%
78%
RAMLEH

100%
RAMALLAH

JERUSALEM

38%
62%

2%
98%
GAZA

Less than 1%

Less than 1%
HEBRON

DEAD SEA

Less than 1%
BEERSHEBA

to support the reconstituted Arab Higher Committee, which the British finally permitted to function again in 1945. The league also set up an agricultural fund to advance credit to Palestinian farmers and thereby curb Zionist land acquisition. In sharp contrast to Zionist strategy, there was a total absence on the Arab side of any military preparedness or planning. The first time the Arab League seriously faced this question was in September 1947, though even then the measures decided on were altogether inadequate. Arab inattention to the military dimension resulted largely from a misplaced belief that Britain would not abdicate its responsibilities as the Mandatory power in Palestine.

But the British were caught at the point of intersecting pressures generated by Washington and the Zionists on the one hand, and the Arab League on the other. They were now harvesting the crop sown with the Balfour Declaration in 1917. Reluctant to crush the Zionist rebellion, and unable to implement either the 1939 White Paper policy (because of Zionist opposition) or partition (because of Palestinian and Arab opposition), they were rapidly reaching the end of their tether. At first they tried to coopt the United States into serious joint decision-making on Palestine as a means of tempering the American bias in favor of Zionism. In November 1945 they suggested the formation of an Anglo-American committee of inquiry as well as another joint team of experts to follow up on the committee's findings. This effort failed, however, because President Truman endorsed only those recommendations of the Anglo-American Committee's report (issued in May 1946) that supported the Zionist viewpoint. And the joint team's plan for a federal solution of the Palestine problem (issued in July 1946), which neither the Arabs nor the Zionists accepted, was dealt a final blow by Truman's endorsement in August 1946 of the Zionist plan for partition. When another plan, put forward in February 1947 by Britain and based on the concept of provincial autonomy, was also rejected by both Zionists and Arabs, the British referred the whole matter to the United Nations.

By now it had become abundantly clear that a partition plan providing for the establishment of a Jewish state in the greater part of Palestine was the only solution acceptable to the Zionists. It had been equally clear for a decade that such a "solution" was abhorrent to the Palestinians for the same reasons that had spurred them to fight their bitter fight against partition in 1937–39. Only Britain stood in the way of a direct collision between the two protagonists.

Meeting in a special session in April and May of 1947, the United Nations General Assembly decided on the dispatch to Palestine of yet another commission of inquiry: the United Nations Special Committee on Palestine (UNSCOP). In September the new committee produced a majority report endorsing partition and a minority report recommending a federal solution. On 29 October 1947 Britain indicated that it would leave Palestine within six months if no settlement agreeable to both Zionists and Palestinians were reached. Britain was getting out of the way.

CHRONOLOGY

1940   February 28: Publication of Land Transfers Regulations, provided for in White Paper of 1939; regulations protect Palestinian land rights against Zionist acquisition.

August: Death of Vladimir Jabotinsky, right-wing founder of Zionist Revisionist movement.

November: British forbid entry of illegal Jewish immigrants into Palestine for security reasons, but accommodate them elsewhere for duration of war.

SS *Patria*, carrying illegal Jewish immigrants to be transferred by British to alternative accommodation outside Palestine blown up by Zionist terrorists; lives of 252 Jews and British police personnel lost.

1942   February: Avraham Stern, founder of Stern Gang, killed by British police.

MV *Struma*, carrying Jewish immigrants from Rumania, blown up and sunk in Black Sea, with loss of 760 lives.

May: Zionist Biltmore Conference, held at Biltmore Hotel in New York and attended by leading Zionists from U.S. and Palestine, formulates new policy of creating "Jewish commonwealth" in whole of Palestine and organizing Jewish army.

December: Members of U.S. Congress and U.S. public figures submit memorandum to President Roosevelt backing Zionist demand for Jewish army.

1943   March: British uncover large-scale network, connected with Haganah, for stealing arms and explosives from British military installations.

March 20: David Ben-Gurion states that end of World War II will be beginning of Zionist struggle in Palestine.

November: Five-year limit on Jewish immigration (due to end in April 1944) stipulated in White Paper of 1939 extended by Britain because 31,000 visas still unused.

1944   January: Stern Gang and Irgun join ranks in campaign of terror against British.

U.S. Congress introduces joint resolution endorsing Biltmore Program.

February 14: Two British policemen shot dead in Haifa by Zionist terrorists.

March 23: Eight British policemen killed in Haifa, Jaffa, Tel Aviv, and Jerusalem by Zionist terrorists.

May: British Labour Party passes resolution recommending that Palestinians be "encouraged" to move out of Palestine to make way for Jewish immigrants.

Summer: Election platforms of U.S. Republican and Democratic parties call for unrestricted Jewish immigration into Palestine and establishment of Jewish commonwealth in whole country.

August 8: Attempt by Zionist terrorists to assassinate High Commissioner Sir Harold MacMichael and Lady MacMichael in Jerusalem fails.

September: British decide to form Jewish Brigade Group (unit larger than normal brigade) within British army; Brigade Group personnel to be recruited from Palestine.

October: British Middle East commander in chief states that Jewish terrorists are "directly impeding the war effort of Great Britain" and "assisting the enemy."

Preparatory Conference on Arab Unity, held in Alexandria, Egypt, and attended by Palestinian representative, proposes formation of Arab state in Palestine in which non-Arab community will have full rights of citizenship.

November 6: Stern Gang terrorists assassinate Lord Walter Moyne, British resident minister of state, in Cairo.

1945   January: U.S. House of Representatives resolves that U.S. shall facilitate unrestricted Jewish immigration to Palestine in order to reconstitute country as Jewish commonwealth.

February 14: President Roosevelt meets King ibn-Saud at Suez Canal and assures him U.S. will make no move hostile to Arab peoples.

March 22: Covenant of League of Arab States, emphasizing Arab character of Palestine, signed in Cairo by representatives of Egypt, Iraq, Lebanon, Saudi Arabia, Syria, Transjordan, and Yemen.

May 8: End of European war.

July 1: On visit to U.S., Ben-Gurion meets with nineteen prominent American Zionists, who pledge to finance purchase in U.S. of military industrial machinery for use of Haganah.

August 31: President Truman asks British Prime Minister Clement Attlee to grant immigration certificates allowing 100,000 Jews into Palestine.

September: Revival of large-scale illegal Zionist immigration into Palestine.

September 2: Surrender of Japan to Allies.

September 28: British policeman killed in Tel Aviv by Zionist terrorists.

October 31: Palestinian railroad lines cut in 242 places; British suspect combined operation by Haganah, Irgun, and Stern Gang.

November 10: Arab League protests, to Britain and U.S., continued Zionist mass immigration into Palestine.

November 13: British Foreign Secretary Ernest Bevin announces in new statement of policy (White Paper of 1945) continued Jewish immigration into Palestine after exhaustion of 1939 White Paper quota; he also proposes formation of Anglo-American Committee of Inquiry.

November 22: New Arab Higher Committee for Palestine formed to replace one disbanded by British in 1937.

November 24: Six Jews killed in clashes with British troops at coastal colony of Givat Haim.

December 5: Arab League secretary general objects to continued Zionist mass immigration into Palestine after exhaustion of 1939 White Paper quota, and inquires what contribution U.S. and Britain are making to relieve postwar Jewish refugee problem in Europe.

December 27: Irgunists kill five British soldiers and policemen in simultaneous attacks in Jerusalem, Jaffa, and Tel Aviv.

1946   January 16: King ibn-Saud of Saudi Arabia and King Farouk of Egypt issue joint statement from Cairo expressing support for Palestinians.

January 19: Irgunist terrorist attack on Central Prison in Jerusalem results in death of two British officers.

February: Palestinians strike in protest against British decision to allow Zionist mass immigration to continue at rate of 1,500 per month in spite of exhaustion of 1939 White Paper quota.

March 6: Anglo-American Committee of Inquiry arrives in Palestine.

March 28: Arab League establishes fund to protect Palestinian farmers against Zionist land acquisition.

April 25: Seven British soldiers killed in Irgunist terrorist attack on military parking lot in Tel Aviv.

May: Anglo-American Committee publishes report recommending admission of 150,000 Jewish immigrants into Palestine and abolition of Land Transfers Regulations, which protected Palestinians against Zionist land acquisition (see 28 February 1940).

Palestinians strike in protest against Anglo-American Committee's recommendations.

Haganah formulates May 1946 Plan.

May 28–29: At their first summit meeting (in Anshas, Egypt) Arab League heads of state declare that continued support by Britain and U.S. of Zionist mass immigration to and land acquisition in Palestine constitutes hostile act against all Arab countries. They call for independence of Palestine and formation of national government that will safeguard rights of all citizens irrespective of race or creed.

June 6: President Truman calls for immediate immigration of 100,000 Jews into Palestine.

June 11–12: Members of Arab League, meeting in Bludan, Syria, adopt secret resolutions warning Britain and U.S. that their continued disregard of Arab rights in Palestine will adversely affect oil and other commercial interests of two countries in Arab world.

June 17: Simultaneous attacks, presumably by Haganah, on eight major railroad and highway bridges.

June 18: Six British officers abducted by Irgunists in Tel Aviv and Jerusalem.

June 29: British forces arrest 2,675 Jews, including four members of Jewish Agency, in retaliation for terrorist attacks.

July 2: President Truman says U.S. will assume responsibility for transporting 100,000 Jewish immigrants to Palestine.

July 22: Irgunists blow up wing of King David Hotel in Jerusalem housing British civilian administration; 91 civilians killed.

July 24: British issue special White Paper on Terrorism in Palestine accusing Jewish Agency of involvement in acts of terrorism with Irgun and Stern Gang.

July 25: British invite Arab and Zionist leaders to enter negotiations on Palestine.

July 31: Anglo-American Conference, meeting in London, proposes federal scheme for solution of Palestine problem known as Morrison-Grady Plan (after British and American chief delegates, respectively); plan rejected by both Arab and Zionist leaders.

August 5: Jewish Agency asks for Jewish state in Palestine comprising area recommended by 1937 Royal (Peel) Commission, plus whole of Negev.

August 14: President Truman forwards to London partition plan for Palestine along lines demanded by Jewish Agency on August 5.

September: Delegates from Arab states to Round Table Conference in London propose unitary state of Palestine, preserving current Arab majority, in which Jews would have full civil rights. Attended by neither Palestinian nor Zionist leaders, conference ends inconclusively.

September 9: British security officer for Tel Aviv killed with his wife when their house blown up by Zionist terrorists.

October 5: President Truman urges immediate substantial Jewish immigration into Palestine.

October 6: Governor Dewey of New York advocates immigration into Palestine of "not 100,000 but several hundred thousand Jews."

October 29: Inner Zionist Council declares that only establishment of Jewish state can solve twin problems of Jewish people and Palestine.

October 30: Two British soldiers and one British policeman killed, and twelve soldiers wounded, in Irgunist bomb attack on Jerusalem railroad station.

November 5: Jewish leaders arrested on 29 June released.

November 9: Four British policemen killed in house booby-trapped by Irgunists.

November 13: Six policemen killed and ten injured in Irgunist terrorist attack on railroad car on Lydda-Jerusalem line.

November 17: Three British policemen killed near Tel Aviv when vehicle mined by Irgunists explodes.

December 2: Four British soldiers killed in military vehicle blown up by land mine planted by Irgunists.

December 4: Jewish Agency Executive appeals for cessation of acts of terrorism by Jews.

December 12: Arab League calls on Britain to arm Palestinians against Zionist terrorist attacks.

December 24: World Zionist Congress, meeting in Basel, decides not to send representatives to London Conference.

December 29: British army officer and three NCOs abducted by Irgunists and flogged in reprisal for flogging of Irgunist terrorist.

1947 January 26: London Round Table Conference reopens.

January 12: Car bomb driven by Irgunists into British administrative headquarters in Haifa kills two British and two Palestinian policemen, and injures more than 100 persons.

January 26: British businessman abducted by Irgunists in Jerusalem.

January 27: British president of district court of Tel Aviv abducted by Irgunists.

January 28–29: Two abducted Britishers released after British issue ultimatum to Irgun.

February 7: British Foreign Secretary Ernest Bevin proposes variant of Morrison-Grady federal plan at London Conference and to Jewish Agency.

February 9–10: Both Jewish Agency and Arab delegations to London Conference reject Bevin's proposal.

February 18: Bevin announces British submission of Palestine problem to United Nations.

February 28: Twenty persons (military, police, and civilian) killed in series of Zionist terrorist attacks, including demolition of British officers' club in Jerusalem.

March 24: Arab League blames Britain and U.S. for deteriorating situation in Palestine.

April 16: Four Zionist terrorists executed in Acre prison.

April 26: British officer and five security personnel killed when car bomb driven by Irgunists into British camp at Sarona, near Tel Aviv.

April 28: UN General Assembly opens special session on Palestine problem.

May 15: UN special session ends with appointment of eleven-member Special Committee on Palestine (UNSCOP), eleventh commission of inquiry appointed since 1919.

May 21: In two simultaneous terrorist attacks near Tel Aviv, Haganah kills two Palestinians and wounds seven.

June 5: Stern Gang claims responsibility for letter bombs addressed to leading British government officials in London.

June 14: UNSCOP members begin arriving in Palestine.

July 20: UNSCOP arrives in Beirut to hear testimony from representatives of Arab states.

July 30: Irgun announces "execution" of two British army sergeants held hostage since July 12.

August 15: Haganah terrorist attack on Palestinian orange grower's house near Tel Aviv kills twelve occupants including mother and six children.

September: Haganah emissaries sent to Czechoslovakia to conclude arms deal with Skoda arms firm.

September 8: Publication of UNSCOP report; majority of members recommend partition, and minority recommend federal solution.

September 16–19: Arab League, meeting in Sofar, Lebanon, appoints Technical Military Committee to supervise Palestinian defense needs, and denounces UNSCOP partition recommendation.

September 26: British Colonial Secretary Arthur Creech Jones announces Britain's decision to terminate Palestine Mandate.

September 29: Arab Higher Committee for Palestine announces rejection of partition.

October 2: Jewish Agency announces acceptance of partition.

October 3: Palestinians call for three-day general strike.

October 7–15: Arab League, meeting in Aley, Lebanon, reaffirms secret Bludan resolutions affecting Western oil interests, and allocates £1,000,000 to Technical Military Committee.

October 11: U.S. endorses partition.

October 13: Soviet Union endorses partition.

October 29: Britain indicates it will leave Palestine in six months if no settlement agreeable to both Zionists and Palestinians reached.

Political Developments

Palestinians Fight the Axis

292 In spite of their bitterness at the brutality of the British suppression of their rebellion, about nine thousand Palestinians volunteered during World War II for service in the British forces against the Axis powers. Some of these volunteers are seen here on parade in Nablus in May 1941.

The Stern Gang Assassinates Lord Moyne

293 Lord Walter Moyne (1880–1944), close friend of Winston Churchill, British colonial secretary in 1941–42, and subsequently minister resident in the Middle East. On 6 November 1944 he was assassinated in Cairo by two members of the terrorist organization Lohemai Herut Israel (Fighters for the Freedom of Israel), otherwise known as the Stern Gang after its founder Avraham Stern. Yitzhak Shamir, former speaker of the Knesset and current prime minister of Israel, was one of the three leaders of the Stern Gang who ordered the assassination.[1]

292

293

The Irgun and Transjordan

294 A poster of the Irgun Zvai Leumi (National Military Organization), "Irgun" for short, which began its terrorist campaign against the Palestinians in September 1937, and was the parent body of the Stern Gang. The Hebrew letters inside the square stand for "the sole solution." This solution, as indicated by the map and the superimposed rifle, was the establishment of Israel by force on both banks of the Jordan River, i.e., in Palestine and Transjordan. The date of the poster is ca. 1946.

Menachem Begin and Vladimir Jabotinsky

295 Menachem Begin, former prime minister of Israel, addressing a rally soon after the establishment of Israel. Note the similarity between the poster shown here and the one in the preceding photograph; the Hebrew words mean "homeland and freedom." Begin arrived in Palestine from the Soviet Union in May 1942 as a member of Polish forces commanded by General Wladyslaw Anders, which were en route to fight the Germans in the West. Begin deserted to join the Irgun (whose leader he soon became) in order to fight the British and later the Palestinians. He opened his terrorist campaign against the British in February 1944, before the final defeat of Hitler. The portrait is of Vladimir Jabotinsky, Begin's rightwing Polish Zionist mentor. Jabotinsky was the leader of Revisionist Zionism, which from the early 1920s called for "revising" the Mandate to enable the Zionists to colonize the East Bank of the Jordan River (Transjordan) as well as Palestine.

IRGUN ZWAÏ LËUMI BE-EREZ JISRAËL

ORGANISATION MILITAIRE NATIONALE JUIVE D'EREZ JISRAËL

JEWISH NATIONAL MILITARY ORGANISATION OF EREZ JISRAËL

An Irgun poster for distribution in Central Europe.

294

296

Zionist Strategic Colonization

296–298 About three hundred Zionist rural colonies, collective and noncollective, were established between 1882 and 1948 in Palestine. Throughout this period, however, the vast majority of the Jewish population (75 percent in 1948) continued to live in the three main cities: Jerusalem, Haifa, and Tel Aviv. Collective colonies (kibbutzim and moshavim) were not introduced until the first decade of this century. Even by 1948 less than 7 percent of Palestine was Jewish-owned, chiefly by the central Zionist land-acquisition organization, the Jewish National Fund (Keren Kayemeth). The sites of many colonies were chosen with geopolitical or military considerations in mind. Some, as in these photographs taken ca. 1946, were straight military strongholds. The bulk of the rural male population, especially in the collective colonies, belonged to the official Zionist military organization, the Haganah (see 308, 394, 409ff.).[2]

Illegal Immigration

299, 300 At the end of World War II, the Zionist leadership decided to undermine the British regime in Palestine as a prelude to the establishment of a Jewish state. One of its chosen tactics was the sponsorship of illegal mass Jewish immigration into the country over and above the official postwar annual quota of 18,000 Jewish immigrants (set by the British in spite of their promise to the Arab delegates at the 1939 London Conference; see 291). Between 1946 and 1948, tens of thousands of illegal immigrants were transported to Palestine from European ports. These scenes were photographed at Haifa in the summer of 1946.

297

298

299

300

301

302

The King David Hotel

301, 302 Another tactic chosen by Zionist leaders was terrorism. On 22 July 1946 Menachem Begin, then head of the Irgun (see 294), ordered the blowing up of the south wing of the King David Hotel in Jerusalem, which housed the central offices of the civilian administration. Ninety-one civil servants and civilian visitors were killed, of whom forty-one were Arab, twenty-eight British, and seventeen Jewish. The frequent use of powerful explosives against civilian targets was first introduced into the Palestine conflict by the Irgun in 1937; it was perfected by the Irgun (to include car bombs) in 1947–48 under Begin.

Arms Dumps in the Zionist Colonies

303, 304 Many of the Zionist colonies (see 296–298) had arms dumps hidden among their civilian population and beneath ostensibly civilian installations. These photographs record the successful outcome of a rare and short-lived British effort in the summer of 1946 to unearth some of them.

303

304

305

306

Arab League Warnings

305 A meeting of the Political Committee of the Arab League in Bludan, Syria, June 1946. The committee expressed concern about the rising tide of Zionist terrorism in Palestine, and protested increasing American support of Zionism.

The Haifa Railroad Station

306 The railroad station at Haifa blown up by Zionist terrorists, fall 1946.

Hostage Taking by the Irgun

307 Hostage taking and sometimes the murder of hostages were two terrorist practices introduced by the Irgun under Menachem Begin. This photograph shows the bodies of two British army sergeants, Clifford Martin (left) and Mervyn Paice. Taken hostage by the Irgun, they were hanged and their bodies booby-trapped to kill the would-be rescuers; July 1947.

The Haganah Starts Its Offensive

308 The farmhouse of the Abu Laban family, prosperous Palestinian orange growers, near Petah Tikva. On 15 August 1947 the house was attacked and blown up by the Haganah, the official Zionist military organization (see 296–298). Twelve occupants, including a mother and six children, were killed. The Palestinians had been quiescent since 1939, and this first major post-World War II terrorist attack by the Haganah was an ominous harbinger of later developments. The Haganah was under the command of David Ben-Gurion. (See 394, 409ff.)

307

308

Views of Towns

309

309 Acre, looking south toward the Old City and the new suburbs beyond. By the end of the Mandate the total population of Acre was ca. 12,360, of whom ca. 50 were Jews and the rest Palestinians. Zionist forces captured the town on 17 May 1948 (see 416–417).

310 The town of Safed in northern Galilee; the round objects in the foreground are "hay cakes" drying in the sun (they were placed under cooking vessels to protect the latter from direct contact with the fire). By the end of the Mandate the total population of Safed was ca. 11,930, of whom ca. 2,400 were Jews and the rest Palestinians. Zionist forces captured the town on 11 May 1948.

311 Houses and terraces of Ramallah. By the end of the Mandate the total population of Ramallah was ca. 5,000, all of whom were Palestinians, the majority Christians. Ramallah was captured by Israel during the 1967 War.

310

311

312

312 The population of Nablus (ca. 23,000 by the end of the Mandate) was entirely Palestinian. The city was captured by Israel in 1967.

313 Hebron, from a balcony. The population of Hebron (ca. 25,000 by the end of the Mandate) was entirely Palestinian. The city was captured by Israel in 1967.

314 Gaza, from Jabal Muntar, 1943. The population of Gaza (ca. 34,000 by the end of the Mandate) was entirely Palestinian. The city was captured by Israel in 1956, and again in 1967.

313

314

315

315 Beit Jala, near Bethlehem, from the air. At the
     end of the Mandate its population was ca. 4,000,
     almost all of whom were Christian Palestinians.
     The village was captured by Israel in 1967.

316

316 The stout sea walls of Acre, originally con-
structed in the ninth century A.D.

317

318

319

317 Gaza's municipality building.

318 The Dajani Private Hospital, Jaffa, built in 1933.

319 Jaffa in the mid-1940s. By the end of the Mandate Jaffa's population was about 100,000, of whom about 30 percent were Jews and the rest Palestinians. Zionist forces captured the city on 10 May 1948 (see 412–415).

320 Close-up of the Alhambra Cinema, Jaffa.

321 The Friends' Boys School, Ramallah, early 1940s.

322 Distinctive local architecture: a villa in Ramallah.

320

321

322

324

323 Main portal of the al-Aqsa Mosque, Jerusalem, 1943.

324 Colonnaded interior of the al-Aqsa Mosque. Note the stained-glass windows.

325 The *mihrab* ("niche pointing in the direction of Mecca") and *minbar* ("pulpit") of the al-Aqsa Mosque.

325

326 Jerusalem street scene outside Jaffa Gate, early 1940s.

327 The Tannous building (owned by a Protestant Palestinian family), West Jerusalem, where much of the property was Palestinian-owned, early 1940s.

328 A house in the Palestinian residential quarter of Talbiyya, West Jerusalem, early 1940s.

326

327

328

329

330

331

329–331 Examples of Palestinian urban architecture, Jerusalem, early 1940s.

332

332 A general view of the Talbiyya quarter, West Jerusalem, early 1940s. In addition to the Talbiyya
quarter, all the other Palestinian residential
quarters of West Jerusalem, e.g., Upper and
Lower Bak'a, Katamon, the German Colony, and
the Greek Colony, were captured by Zionist
forces on 30 April 1948.

Trades and Industry

The Jewish community in Palestine enjoyed enormous advantages over the Palestinians in the industrial sphere. These advantages included capital in the form of financial contributions from Jewish communities overseas, highly skilled manpower in the form of professional Jewish immigration into the country, and industrial plants made available not only through access to industrial capital but also because restrictions prevailing in Germany allowed Jewish capitalists wishing to settle in Palestine to transfer their assets in kind only. Other factors favoring the Jewish community in the industrial sphere were its class structure (largely urban middle-class), its centralized political institutions, and British protectionism. Thus in every field of industrial endeavor, the Jewish community predominated. But Palestinian traditional industries (particularly the production of edible oil and the manufacture of soap) were vigorous, and Palestinians were increasingly active in the tobacco, textile, wood products, cement, and paper industries.

333 The Arab Fair when it was first held in Jerusalem, 1933.

334 The Iraqi pavilion at the Arab Fair, 1933.

335 The ancient craft of soapmaking.

336 Wrapping soap in the Hassan Shak'ah factory, Nablus, ca. 1940.

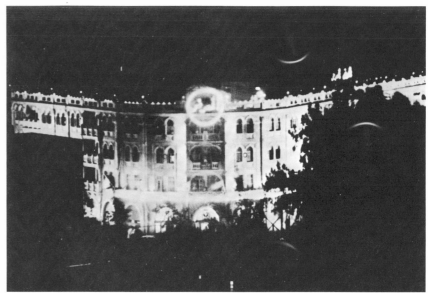

333

334

335

336

337 Trimming boot soles, 1942.

338 The Na'meh flour mills, Nablus, 1940.

339 The machine room at the Na'meh flour mills, Nablus.

340 Match factory, Nablus, 1940.

337

338

339

340

341 Bales of Tatli-Sert tobacco in storage, Nazareth,
ca. 1940.

342 The packaging of cigarettes at the Arab Cigarette
and Tobacco Company, Nazareth, ca. 1940.

341

342

342a–342q A collage of advertisements.

The ARAB BANK Ltd.

It is the first ARAB BANK established in Palestine with, Capital purely subscribed by Arabs, and it is altogether managed by Arab hands. It enjoyed the utmost confidence and success owing to the co-operation of the Arab Nationalists both at Home and in America. Its customers were multiplied in number; and it established two branches, one in Jaffa and the other in Haifa, while a third branch will be shortly established at Amman.

The Bank receives short term and long term deposits; with a high rate of interest. It gives credit on commercial and financial papers. It discounts Commercial Bills whether they are sight or time drafts. It accepts Promissory Notes on collection and issues Inland and Foreign Checks. It buyes Financial Papers and different Notes of the Foreign currencies. In general it performs all the Banking Business.

Its moto in its work, has always been, Righteousness, faithfulness, and sincerity. Its stimulus is work and perseverence.

We, therefore request every Arab and Nationalist to serve his country by dealing with this Bank and co-operating with it for Nations are never built without Co-operation.

342a

Arab Citrus Line, Jaffa

The Arab-Line for Jaffa Citrus Fruits, is the unique national Arab Company, was formed two years ago for the purpose of shipping Jaffa oranges. It has a board consisted of 8 merchants whose duties are: To fix ships' destinations & to classify & designate sale-market.

The shipment charges of this company since its being established have been 1 S. 2 d. per box, whereas the fees of other Companies are 1 S. 7 d. The 5 d. difference is economized to the interest of the shipper.

342b

شركة برتقال يافا

يافا ـ شارع اسكندر عوض رقم ٨   تلفون ١٤١٦ ـ ص. ب ٢٨٩

لاصحابها :

توفيق واحمد ابو ابن وشركاهم

تنتج وتصدر جميع انواع الاثمار الحمضية لعموم الاقطار المجاورة وما وراء البحار وخاصة المملكة المتحدة ومن اشهر ماركاتها المسجلة :

GOLD-APPLE	GOLD-BEAM
J. O. C.	DIANA
TOP-DOG	HEROS
GOLD-KIST	ABDULLA

JAFFA ORANGE Co.

JAFFA, Haward Street No. 8   Telephone 1416   P. O. B. 289

Props. : T. & A. ABU-LABAN & CO.

Growers & Exporters of all kind of Citrus Fruits to all parts of near by countries & Europe, especially U. K.

Its famous registered brands :

GOLD-APPLE	GOLD-BEAM
J. O. C.	DIANA
TOP-DOG	HEROS
GOLD-KIST	ABDULLA

342c

THE JAFFA PRESS CO.

JAFFA, Birket Kamar St.   P. O. Box 132.   Teleph. 1078.   Teleg. : JAPCO.

بيع وطبع
ورق اف الاثمار الحمضية
***
طبع
صناديق البرتقال الخشبية
***
مطبوعات تجارية على اختلافها
بجميع الالوان واللغات
***
معمل لصنع وطبع
اكياس الورق
***

Merchants & Printers of Citrus Fruits Wrapping Paper
***
Printers of Citrus Fruits Wood Cases
***
Commercial Printing Multi-Colours in all Languages
***
Manufacturers and Printers of Paper Bags

تلفون ١٠٧٨ ـ ص. ب ١٣٢ ـ تلغرافيا «جابكو» يافا

342d

275

276

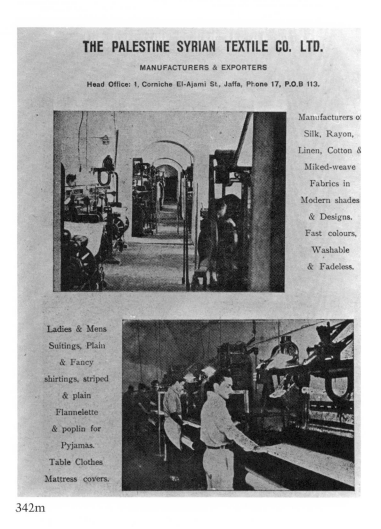

278

Disributors

Jerusalem

P.O. [Box 278]

Phone: 1340 / 8

Shukri Deeb

342p

الوكلاء المعتمدون

القدس

صندوق البريد ٢٧٨

تلفون ١٣٤٠ / ٨

شكري ديب

شركة السكب الفلسطينية

المحدودة الاسهم

يافا ــ شارع القدس تلفون ٧٧١

١ تأسست سنة ١٩٣١ لسد حاجة عرب فلسطين الى مؤسسة وطنية تتولى صنع ما يحتاج اليه المصانع والمؤسسات العربية في البلاد .

٢ تصنع الشركة ، في معاملها الخاصة ، أجزاء الموتورات والماكينات وقواعد « شاسي » لموتورات ديزل البحرية ، والطلمبات والمكابس والكسارات والطواحين وغيرها من الأدوات الميكانيكية الممتازة الدقيقة الصنع .

٣ لدى الشركة كل التجهيزات العصرية اللازمة لصهر الحديد وسكبه وخراطته وتجهيزه وإخراجه آلات حديثة ، دقيقة الصنع ، متينة .

٤ في الشركة تسعون عامل عربي فني يقومون بهذه الأعمال الدقيقة تحت اشراف مدير عام هو السيد موسى عبدالنبي ، خريج جامعة لويزيانا في الولايات المتحدة الاميركية .

PALESTINE IRON AND BRASS FOUNDRY LTD.

Jerusalem Road, JAFFA — Tel. 771

An Arab institution founded in 1931 by Arab industrialists who appreciated the importance of mechanised industry in the economic future of the country.

It has since helped to cover the ever increasing need for Hydraulic Press, Pumps, Stone Crushers, Irrigation Blunger Pumps, Flour Mills etc.

The Palestine Iron and Brass Foundry Company employs ninty skilled Arab workers highly experienced. The Company has succeeded into securing customers even from Transjordan, Syria and Lebanon.

The Palestine Iron and Brass Foundry Company is actually the largest of its kind in Palestine.

Opposite : Samples of mechanised articles produced by the Company for use in industrial, agricultural and all sorts of constructive shemes in Palestine.

342q

343

343 Faidi al-Alami with his wife and son Musa, Jerusalem, 1919 (see 67). Musa received a law degree from Cambridge University. During the 1930s he was junior crown counsel in the Mandatory administration, and for a brief period served as private secretary to the British high commissioner. In 1939 he was a member of the Palestine delegation to the London Conference (see 291). Musa represented the Palestinian political parties at the Preparatory Conference, held in Alexandria in 1944, preceding the establishment in 1945 of the League of Arab States. At his suggestion, the conference agreed to set up Arab information offices in several European capitals as well as in New York, and to create a special fund to help Palestinian farmers retain their land. After 1948 Musa founded the Arab Development Society, which (among other projects) established and ran a model agricultural training school for boys, in Jericho.

344 Reverend Salih Saba and family, Jerusalem, ca. 1922. Fuad Saba (standing first left) was the first Palestinian licensed auditor to practice under the British Mandate. By 1948 the F. Saba Company had branches in Transjordan, Syria, Lebanon, Iraq, and Egypt. Fuad was one of the members of the Arab Higher Committee who was exiled to the Seychelles Islands (see 242, 268–269), and he attended the 1939 London Conference (see 291).

345 Schoolmasters, Jaffa, ca. 1923. Seated is Thabit al-Khalidi, author of a chemistry textbook, who became Jordanian ambassador to the United Nations and later to Iran. Standing (left to right) are Wasfi Anabtawi, author of several geography textbooks and later minister of finance in Jordan; Sami al-Eid, later headmaster of a school in Acre; and Salim Katul (see 211–212).

344

345

346

346 A prominent Muslim family, Jaffa, mid-1920s.

347 Guard of the United States Consulate in Jerusalem in the traditional costume of the *qawwas*
("consular guard").

348 Dr. Daoud Bulos, a Protestant medical doctor,
with his wife Adla and son Nasib (later a lawyer), Acre, 1923.

349 The two young men in the front row of this photograph are left, Akram Zu'aiter (see 233, 235)
and right, Ahmad Shukairi (see 69, 105, 224).

347

349

348

350

351

350 Hashim al-Jayyusi (1901–81), mayor of Tulkarm from 1939 to 1948 (see 376). Subsequently, he served six times as Jordanian minister of finance and was acting prime minister and deputy speaker of the Senate in Jordan.

351 Villagers from Deir Yassin, 1927. Building contractor Haj Ahmad al-As'ad with his son Muhammad, his wife (resting her hand on his shoulder), and a relative. (See 411)

352 Raghib al-Nashashibi (see 100, 196, 242), an outstanding public figure under the Ottoman Empire, the British Mandate, and the Jordanian administration. He began his career as head of the Ottoman Department of Public Works, and then represented Jerusalem in the Ottoman Parliament during World War I. From 1920 to 1934 he was mayor of Jerusalem. He formed and led the Defense Party, which he represented on the Arab Higher Committee (see 242). Generally considered a moderate in his opposition to the British Mandate, he became custodian of the holy places of Jerusalem after the 1948 War, under Jordanian rule.

353 Faridah Dumyan, Haifa, 1931.

352

353

354

355

356

357

358

354 Mrs. Tawfiq Bisisu with her children, Gaza, 1933. Proudly holding a magazine is Mu'in, later a poet and playwright closely associated with the Palestine Liberation Organization (PLO).

355 Palestine's poet laureate, Ibrahim Tuqan, a graduate of the American University of Beirut; Nablus, 1934. From 1936 to 1941 Tuqan was in charge of the Arabic section of the Palestine Broadcasting Station.

356 Three playmates, Haifa, 1934.

357 Khalil Baydas from Nazareth (1874–1949), Russian scholar and pioneer of the modern Palestinian novel. As early as 1898, he had translated some of the works of Tolstoy and Pushkin into Arabic. Khalil was the father of Yusuf Baydas, a Palestinian banker.

358 Adil Zu'aiter (see 102) with his two sons, Wa'il (on his lap) and Umar, Nablus, 1935. Umar became an artillery officer in Kuwait. As the PLO representative in Rome, Wa'il was assassinated there by Israeli intelligence agents in 1972.

359

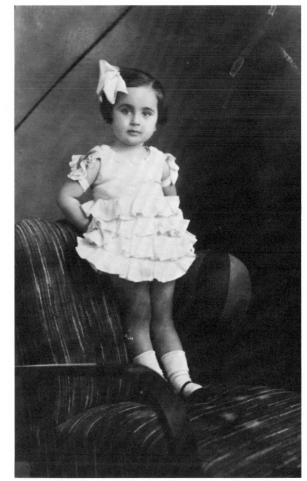

360

361

359 Hasan Sidqi al-Dajani, a Jerusalem journalist, lawyer, and politician. As legal counsel to the Palestinian Union of Drivers, he organized the strike by the transport sector in 1936 at the beginning of the Great Rebellion (see 242ff.).

360 Muna Asfour, later married to architect Bahij Saba (now an American citizen), Haifa, 1937.

361 Charlotte Jallad (center) from Jaffa, with friends on a trip to the Dead Sea, 1937.

362 A predominantly Palestinian group of political science students at the American University of Beirut, 1937.

363 Palestinian author Asma Tubi from Nazareth (on arm of chair); and Safiyyah Riyahi from Jaffa (seated), who became a lecturer in Arabic at Beirut College for Women; 1938.

364

364 After graduating from Cambridge University,
George Antonius (1891–1942) began his civil service career in Palestine first in the Education
Department and then in the Secretariat (the British Mandatory Executive). He resigned from the
latter in 1930 to become Middle Eastern associ-
ate of the Institute of Current World Affairs in
New York. His classic book, *The Arab Awaken-
ing*, was published by Hamish Hamilton of London in 1938. Antonius was secretary general to
the Arab delegations at the London Conference,
1939 (see 291).

365

365 An unidentified Christian Orthodox bishop, ca. 1939.

366

367

366 Shepherds and a schoolmaster, with their respective flocks, cross paths outside the Church of All Nations, Gethsemane.

367 The "oriental band" (*takht*) of the Palestine Broadcasting Station entertaining guests at a private party, Jerusalem, 1940.

368

369

368 Girl Guides of the Government Girls' School in Nazareth, 1940.

369 Dancing in the gymnasium, Jerusalem Girls' College, early 1940s.

370

371

370 A Jerusalem postman making his rounds.

371 Performers in *The Merchant of Venice* at the Friends' Boys School, Ramallah, ca. 1941. Sa'id Abu Hamdeh, later a professional photographer, is first right.

372 The English Debating Society of the Najah (Success) School, Nablus, 1942. Isam Abbasi (standing second from right) became a poet and novelist as well as literary contributor to *al-Ittihad*, a newspaper in Haifa.

373 Ruth Raad, daughter of photographer Khalil Raad, in the traditional costume of Ramallah, ca. 1943. (See 72, 124–136, 186)

372

373

374 Moghannam Moghannam, an American-educated Protestant lawyer from Ramallah in the "oriental" room of his house, ca. 1944. He was secretary of the Seventh Palestinian National Congress (see 82), and later secretary general of the Defense Party. (For his wife, see 93.)

375 Troopers of the TJFF (Transjordanian Frontier Force), recruited mostly from among Palestinians, prepare to leave for London to attend victory celebrations at the end of World War II. The British disbanded the force (some 2,500 strong) several months before the end of the Mandate (see 256).

376 Fourth Conference of the Arab Mayors of Palestine, Gaza, 1945. In the front row, left to right, are Hashim al-Jayyusi (see 350), Rushdi al-Shawwa (Gaza), Omar Bitar (Jaffa), Shaikh Mustafa al-Khairi (Ramleh), and Suleiman Tuqan (Nablus). In the center, second row, is Shaikh Muhammad Ali al-Ja'bari (Hebron) and, to his right, Hanna Qawwas (Bethlehem). There were eighteen Palestinian municipal councils, two Jewish councils, and four mixed councils under the Mandate.

377 Aliyyah al-Khairi bathing her son Fawwaz (now an airline pilot), Wadi Hunayn, near Ramleh, 1945.

374

375

376

377

Studio Venus
Amman

378

379

380

378 Leaders of the Arab Protestant community of
Palestine, 1946. Reverend Butrus Nasir from Bir
Zeit is seated third from left. His nephew Kamal
Nasir, the late poet and member of the Execu-
tive Committee of the Palestine Liberation Or-
ganization (PLO), was assassinated with two
other PLO leaders in an Israeli raid on Beirut in
April 1973.

379 Wajidah Taji, Wadi Hunayn, near Ramleh, 1946.
Wajidah became principal aide to Musa al-Alami
(see 343) at the Boys' Farm in Jericho, run by the
Arab Development Society.

380 Muslim dignitaries conferring in the courtyard of
the Ibrahimi (Abraham) Mosque, Hebron, 1947
(see 180). The mayor of Hebron, Shaikh Muhammad Ali al-Ja'bari, is on the right.

381

382

381 The board of directors and some members of the Arab Architects' and Engineers' Association of Jerusalem at the Church of the Nativity, Bethlehem, 1947. George Shibr (sixth right), a Protestant, was an architect for the Awqaf (Muslim Religious Endowments) Administration; he undertook the restoration of the Nabi Samu'il (the prophet Samuel) Mosque north of Jerusalem, and the Ibrahimi (Abraham) Mosque in Hebron.

382 Dr. Nimr Tuqan, a pathologist and brilliant mimic from Nablus, with nurses at the Haifa Government Hospital, 1947. The brother of Ibrahim Tuqan (see 355), he became chief pathologist at the American University Hospital in Beirut.

383

384

383 Choir practice at the Women's Teachers' Training College, Jerusalem, spring 1947.

384 Boarders at Schmidt Girls' College in the orange orchards of Jericho, 1947.

385

386

385 Wedding portrait of Dr. Jabra al-A'raj and his
bride, Lydia, Beit Jala, ca. 1947.

386 Anton Attallah, judge in the district courts of Jerusalem and Haifa (1939–43), deputy mayor of Jerusalem (1944–46), and minister of foreign affairs
for Jordan (1963–67).

PART V

CIVIL WAR AND THE DESTRUCTION OF THE PALESTINIAN COMMUNITY

NOVEMBER 1947–MAY 1948

INTRODUCTION

THE Palestine problem was now rapidly approaching its catastrophic climax. On 29 November 1947 the United Nations General Assembly passed a resolution recommending the partition of Palestine into a Jewish state, a Palestinian state, and a special international regime (*corpus separatum*) for Jerusalem and its environs; an economic union would be set up between the Jewish and Palestinian states. The Palestinians and other Arabs were as stunned as the Zionists and their sympathizers were jubilant. The very reactions of each side belied the claim that partition was a compromise solution.

PALESTINIAN OPPOSITION TO PARTITION

The member states that championed and endorsed partition did so in the full knowledge of bitter Palestinian and Arab opposition to it. The Palestinians had lost some four thousand lives fighting partition from 1937 to 1939. Since its creation the Arab League had been warning against partition. The UN partition plan was based on the Zionist plan that President Truman had endorsed as early as August 1946. From the Palestinian perspective, partition was Zionist in provenance and conception, and tailored to meet Zionist needs and demands. That the UN resolution won 33 votes to 13, with 10 abstentions and one delegation absent, was largely due to the enormous pressure brought to bear by the United States (including the personal intervention of President Truman) on member states to vote for it. To be sure, the Soviet Union voted for partition also, but only in order to end British rule in Palestine. Significantly, no African or Asian state voted in favor except Liberia and the Philippines. India, Pakistan, Turkey, and Afghanistan all voted against, while China abstained. Many Latin American countries (including Mexico) abstained. Even the Canadian representative was heard to say that his country supported partition "with a heavy heart and many misgivings."[1] The United Kingdom coyly abstained.

Partition was seen by the Palestinians as imposing unilateral and intolerable sacrifices on themselves. The reasons for their opposition were the same as in 1937, except that the UN partition plan gave the proposed Jewish state 50 percent more territory than the 1937 plan had. The area of the Jewish state according to the UN plan would actually be larger than that of the proposed Palestinian state (5,500 square miles as compared with 4,500 square miles) at a time when the Jews constituted no more than 35 percent of the population and owned less than 7 percent of the land. Within the proposed Jewish state, Jewish landownership did not in fact exceed 600 square miles out of the total area of 5,500 square miles. Nearly all the citrus land (equally divided in ownership between Jews and Palestinians), 80 percent of the cereal land (entirely Palestinian-owned), and 40 percent of Palestinian industry would fall within the borders of the proposed Jewish state. Jaffa, the Palestinian state's major port on the Mediterranean, would be altogether cut off from its hinterland, and Gaza would lose its traditional links with the wheatlands of the Negev. Hundreds of villages would be separated from communal fields and pastures. The Palestinian state would lose direct access both to the Red Sea and to Syria. The economic union between the two states, on which partition had been postulated, was known beforehand to be impracticable. The patchwork of subunits into which partition would divide the country bore little relationship to the human and social realities on the ground.

The Palestinians failed to see why they should

be made to pay for the Holocaust (the ultimate crime against humanity, committed in Europe by Europeans), and recalled that Zionism was born in the 1880s, long before the advent of the Third Reich. They failed to see why it was *not* fair for the Jews to be a minority in a unitary Palestinian state, while it *was* fair for almost half of the Palestinian population — the indigenous majority on its own ancestral soil — to be converted overnight into a minority under alien rule in the envisaged Jewish state according to partition.

The injustice of the UN partition resolution was further exposed in Palestinian and Arab eyes by the General Assembly's rejection of relevant draft resolutions proposed by the Arab delegates before the vote on partition. The Arab delegates pleaded that the International Court of Justice be consulted on whether the General Assembly was "competent to enforce or recommend the enforcement" of partition against the wishes of the majority of a country's population. The draft resolution to that effect was defeated in the Ad Hoc Committee by a 21 to 20 vote. Another draft resolution, proposing that all UN member states participate in alleviating the plight of Jewish refugees in Europe "in proportion to their area, economic resources . . . and other relevant factors," was not carried in a 16 to 16 vote (with 25 abstentions). In the circumstances the Palestinians and other Arabs felt that they were not bound by the partition resolution, which in any case was a nonmandatory recommendation by the General Assembly.

ZIONIST PREPARATIONS FOR WAR

As early as May 1942 the Zionist leadership had begun preparations to convert the whole of Palestine into a Jewish state, a policy embodied in the Biltmore Program. The Zionists were all the more capable of implementing a plan envisaging a Jewish state in part (albeit the greater part) of Palestine, i.e., partition. They had paid careful attention to the balance of power between themselves and the Palestinians. They had evolved strategies to offset and diminish the Palestinian quantitative advantage, and had foreseen a sequence of stages leading to the desired revolution in the local status quo. The classic exposition of these policies was made in 1932 by Chaim Arlo-

soroff, director of the Political Department in the Jewish Agency Executive.[2] The European background of the Zionist immigrants and the Zionist leadership's ability to tap the professional, diplomatic, and financial resources of the Jewish communities in the industrialized Western countries stood the Zionist venture in good stead. By 1944 the government statistician in the Palestine administration could say: "The Jewish economy of Palestine is . . . radically different from the Arab economy and is in fact not very dissimilar from that of the United Kingdom."[3]

Military organization was a high Zionist priority. The main armed force was the Haganah (Defense) under the command of the Jewish Agency. The Haganah had evolved in the early days of the Mandate as an offshoot of the pre-Mandatory Hashomer (Watchman), itself descended from the secret societies of Czarist Russia. In 1947 the Haganah had had a continuous existence of at least thirty years. Although officially it was a secret, illegal paramilitary organization, the British not only tolerated the Haganah but assisted it both directly and indirectly. The 14,000-man Jewish Settlement Police, for example, a force trained and supported by the British, became virtually the training cadre for Haganah reservists. By 1946 the Haganah had grown into a relatively formidable force; the Anglo-American Committee reported Haganah strength to be about 62,000. In spite of repeated acts of Zionist terrorism (including Haganah attacks) against British security forces, Britain left the Haganah unscathed. So self-confident was the Haganah command that, in a memorandum submitted to the Anglo-American Committee on 25 March 1946 in Jerusalem, it said:

As far as the strength of the Arabs in Palestine is concerned, we are in possession of well-founded information. There is no doubt that the Jewish force is superior in organization, training, planning and equipment, and that we ourselves will be able to handle any attack or rebellion from the Arab side without calling for any assistance from the British or Americans. If you accept the Zionist solution [partition and a Jewish state in the greater part of Palestine] but are unable or unwilling to enforce it, please do not interfere, and we ourselves will secure its implementation.[4]

PALESTINE

V. United Nations partition recommendation, 29 November 1947.

■ Proposed Palestinian state

■ Proposed Jewish state

This map is based on the map published in George Kirk, *Survey of International Affairs: The Middle East, 1945–1950* (New York: Oxford University Press, 1954), p. 339.

According to the partition recommendation, Jaffa was to be part of the proposed Palestinian state, even though it lay outside the boundaries of that state. Jerusalem and Bethlehem were conceived as a *corpus separatum* under UN jurisdiction.

MEDITERRANEAN SEA

LEBANON

LAKE HULEH

Acre

Safed

SYRIA

Haifa

Tiberias

LAKE TIBERIAS

Nazareth

Beisan

Tulkarm

TRANSJORDAN

Qalqilyah

Tel Aviv

Jaffa

Lydda
Ramleh

Jerusalem
and
Bethlehem

DEAD SEA

Gaza

Beersheba

NEGEV

EGYPT

Aqaba

The Zionist leadership began detailed military planning as early as 1945 in anticipation of the coming showdown. In a statement to his biographer, David Ben-Gurion confirmed that "the major preparations to convert Haganah into an army were begun three years before the birth of the state."[5] On a special visit to the United States in 1945, Ben-Gurion (then chairman of the Jewish Agency Executive), called together nineteen leading American Jewish figures and persuaded them to contribute to the wholesale purchase of military industrial machinery being sold as scrap at the end of the war. The machinery was smuggled into Palestine under the Mandate and became the nucleus of a heavy Jewish military industry.

In May 1946 the Haganah developed a strategy embodied in the so-called May 1946 Plan, in which the central concept was that of "counteraction." Such action was to be of two kinds: "warning" action generally confined to the area of the enemy's own operation, and "punitive" action unrestricted in its geographical scope. Because of inherent "difficulties," counteraction would not always be aimed at the specific Palestinian perpetrators of a previous action. Therefore, the human targets to be sought should be Palestinian political and military leaders, those who financed them, and those who incited them ("e.g., journalists") in addition to those who had carried out actual operations. The objective should be to "inflict physical harm," take the individuals in question "hostage," or "liquidate them." The material targets should be "clubs, cafés, and other meeting places, communication centers, flour mills, water plants and other vital economic installations." Villages, urban residential quarters, and farms used for planning operations or as bases for attack and withdrawal should be surrounded and occupied. "Everything possible in them should be burned and the houses of those who had incited or participated in operations should be blown up."[6]

Soon after the UN partition decision, work began on a new plan, Plan Dalet (D). The objective of Plan Dalet was to take over and control the area of the proposed Jewish state. "It was obvious," in the words of Haganah historians, "that no Jewish colony outside the Jewish state — according to the UN partition resolution — would

be abandoned or vacated and that the Haganah would do everything to organize their resistance." Within the Jewish state proper, Palestinian villages that resisted "should be destroyed . . . and their inhabitants expelled beyond the borders of the Jewish state." A similar strategy would be applied to the towns. "Palestinian residents of urban quarters which dominate access to or egress from the towns should be expelled beyond the borders of the Jewish state in the event of their resistance." Outside the Jewish state, towns such as Qalqilyah and Tulkarm should be occupied; Acre, Nazareth, Lydda, Ramleh, Bethlehem, Beit Jala, and Hebron should all be put under siege. "The inhabitants of Jaffa should be imprisoned within their municipal boundaries and not dare to leave them." All the villages between Tel Aviv and Jerusalem should be occupied. All the Palestinian quarters of West and East Jerusalem, as well as all the environs of the city, should be conquered.[7]

PALESTINIAN AND ARAB COUNTERMEASURES

On their side, the Palestinians had to start from scratch in reorganizing themselves. The 1946 report of the Anglo-American Committee, which estimated Zionist military strength to be ca. 62,000, made no mention of Palestinian military forces. The Palestinians looked to the Arab League to counterbalance Zionist military preponderance. But the league suffered from the constraints and divisiveness already noted.[8] Its first tentative move to meet Palestinian defense needs was made in September 1947 when it formed the Technical Military Committee, headed by an Iraqi former chief of staff, General Ismail Safwat, to report on Palestinian defense requirements. Safwat's first report, submitted on October 8, was somber and realistic. He accurately assessed Zionist strength and asserted that the Palestinians possessed nothing remotely comparable to the Zionist forces "in manpower, organization, armament or ammunition." Urging the Arab states to "mobilize their utmost strength" promptly and form a general command, he warned that the Palestinians were in dire straits. The only Arab League reaction to Safwat's urgings was the allocation on October 15 of one million pounds sterling to the Technical Committee. On November 27, just before the UN partition vote, Safwat again warned: "It is well nigh impossible to overcome the Zionist forces with irregulars. . . . the Arab countries cannot afford a long war. . . ." He pleaded with the Arab countries to "ensure superiority in numbers and matériel and act with maximal speed."

The Arab League was loath to confront Britain, which had emphasized that it would remain solely responsible for the administration of Palestine until the end of the Mandate on 15 May 1948. At the same time a certain wishful thinking prevailed in many Arab capitals (a lingering residue of trust in Western liberalism) that somehow the justice of the Palestinian cause would be recognized and the Western powers would not allow the worst to befall the Palestinians. But with the rapidly deteriorating security situation in Palestine, the Arab countries could no longer postpone action, particularly after the UN partition resolution.

In December 1947 the Arab League decided to supply the Technical Military Committee with ten thousand rifles and to put at its disposal a force of three thousand irregulars. The latter were to form a volunteer Arab Liberation Army (ALA) composed of members from various Arab countries, among them five hundred from Palestine. After training in Damascus, ALA contingents would be sent to the threatened Palestinian areas. The formation of the ALA was the Arab League's compromise measure between exclusive reliance on diplomacy and Western good intentions on the one hand, and the serious action urged by Safwat on the other.

Since the UN partition vote in November, fighting had been escalating dramatically in Palestine. By January 1948 the Irgun and the Stern Gang had introduced the use of car bombs (originally directed against the British), and by March 1948 Palestinian irregulars were paying their opponents back in kind. Haganah attacks on villages and residential quarters were answered by Palestinian attacks on Zionist colonies, and vice versa. By 10 January 1948 the number of killed and wounded on both sides stood at 1,974.

Although militarily inferior, the Palestinians resisted firmly. This was partly a measure of their desperation and partly an effect of the infiltration from Syria of small ALA contingents during the period from January to March, which bolstered Palestinian strength and raised morale. But the real reason for the Palestinians' ability to hold their ground was that the military operations of the Haganah were still being conducted within the framework of the May 1946 Plan, i.e., the Zionist leadership had not begun to implement Plan Dalet. The Zionists were inhibited from doing so primarily because Plan Dalet required a high degree of Haganah mobilization, and the greater its mobilization the greater the chances of a confrontation with Britain, which claimed to be the de jure authority throughout the country until May 15.

Meanwhile, the appearance of a military stalemate in Palestine, the rising casualties on both sides, and the increasing involvement of ALA units in the fighting were having a considerable political impact in Washington and at the United Nations. A trend away from partition began to crystallize in March in the form of a call by the Truman administration for the General Assembly to reconsider the partition plan and to recommend the installation of a trusteeship regime instead. The American proposal created great alarm among the Zionists, who bitterly denounced it. Their alarm was all the greater because their line of communication with President Truman, their paramount champion, had broken down.

TRUMAN INTERVENES

For several months Truman had refused to meet with any American Zionist leader as a result of the intense pressure exerted on him by American Zionists since the partition resolution. How intense this pressure must have been to so alienate Truman is perhaps indicated by the fact that 1948 was a presidential election year. On March 8 Truman declared his own candidacy in the presidential elections. On March 18 he finally agreed to meet the veteran British Zionist leader Chaim Weizmann. Weizmann had been sent to the United States by the Zionist leadership in Palestine for precisely this kind of contact, at the highest level of government.

The meeting between Truman and Weizmann took place secretly at the White House. Although Truman had approved his State Department's recommendation of trusteeship, he may not have fully grasped its implications. The Zionists were at a crossroads. There were only two months to go until the end of the Mandate. If the trusteeship proposal (which the Arab League accepted) received the full backing of the American president, this could mean the indefinite postponement of the establishment of the Jewish state. Moreover, Plan Dalet had been completed and was awaiting implementation. British evacuation was progressing steadily, as was Zionist military mobilization. The end of the Mandate on May 15 would leave a juridical vacuum, which the Arab countries could use to their advantage. The Jewish state had to be made an accomplished fact before then. But without the implementation of Plan Dalet, the Jewish state could not be established. What the Zionist leaders needed to know at first hand was the American president's own attitude toward the establishment of a Jewish state in these circumstances.

President Truman did not disappoint Weizmann. As he informs us in his memoirs: "When he [Weizmann] left my office I felt that he had reached a full understanding of my policy and that I knew what he wanted."[9] And as Abba Eban confirms: "The President gave his visitor a specific commitment. He would work for the establishment and recognition of a Jewish state of which the Negev would be a part."[10] There can be little doubt that Weizmann promptly sent the news to Tel Aviv and that the Zionist leadership there had little difficulty in understanding its significance.

On March 19, the day after the Truman-Weizmann meeting, the United States chief delegate to the United Nations Security Council, Warren Austin, unaware of this meeting and its outcome, proposed that action be suspended on the partition plan and the General Assembly convene to discuss the trusteeship solution. The Arab countries, equally unaware of the Truman-Weizmann meeting, welcomed with relief the American trusteeship proposal, and the Arabic press celebrated the occasion. But Safwat, chairman of the Military Committee, in command of the Arab Liberation Army, had no such illusions. With his eyes on the ground in Palestine, he warned on March 23: "The operational initiative in most of Palestine is in Zionist hands. . . . Our relatively stronger garrisons in Jaffa, Jerusalem, and Haifa are strictly on the defensive. . . ."

PLAN DALET

Plan Dalet went into effect during the first week of April. Its many subsidiary operations continued to unfold with devastating cumulative impact during the remaining six weeks of the Mandate. Some of these operations dovetailed with one another in a single region. Others took place concurrently in different parts of the country. Psychological offensives designed to induce civilians to flee were orchestrated with the military operations; the former involved broadcasting by radio or loudspeakers (carried in vehicles) and spreading rumors by word of mouth or leaflets.

Six major operations were launched in April. Two of them, Operations Nachshon (April 5–15) and Harel (April 15–20), were designed to occupy and destroy the Palestinian villages along the whole length of the Jaffa-Jerusalem road, thus splitting in two the central mass (according to the UN partition plan) of the Palestinian state. Palestinian villagers and irregulars fought desperately along the entire highway. A dramatic battle developed for the hilltop village of Castel, some five miles west of Jerusalem. The Palestinians fought under their charismatic commander Abd al-Qadir al-Husseini, and the village changed hands several times. Abd al-Qadir was killed on April 9 as he led a successful counterattack. While the Castel battle was in progress, Irgun and Stern Gang units perpetrated the massacre of 245 civilian inhabitants of the village of Deir Yassin, about three miles from Castel. The Deir Yassin massacre was one of the more gruesome instances of "competition" between the Labour-dominated Haganah (in charge of Plan Dalet) and the right-wing Revisionist Irgun. Meanwhile, the ALA field commander, Fawzi al-Qawukji, opened a diversionary attack against the colony of Mishmar Haemek, southeast of Haifa; the attack was

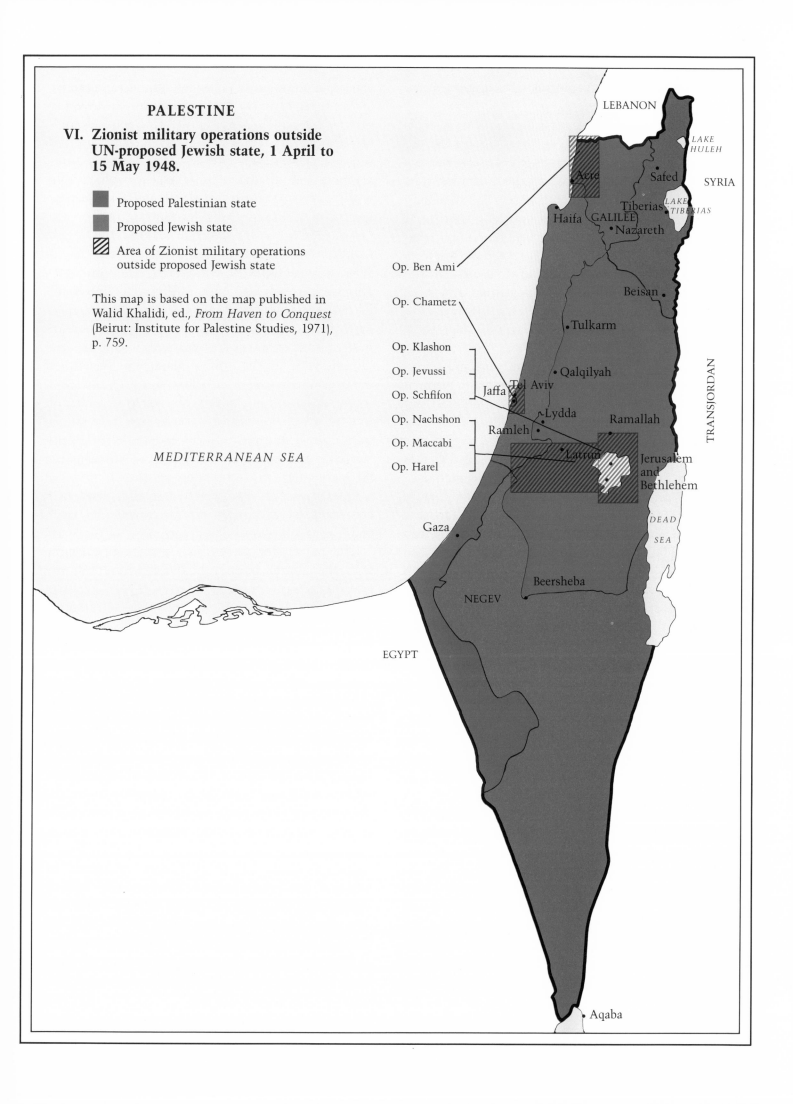

PALESTINE

VI. Zionist military operations outside UN-proposed Jewish state, 1 April to 15 May 1948.

Proposed Palestinian state

Proposed Jewish state

Area of Zionist military operations outside proposed Jewish state

This map is based on the map published in Walid Khalidi, ed., *From Haven to Conquest* (Beirut: Institute for Palestine Studies, 1971), p. 759.

MEDITERRANEAN SEA

Op. Ben Ami

Op. Chametz

Op. Klashon

Op. Jevussi

Op. Schfifon

Op. Nachshon

Op. Maccabi

Op. Harel

LEBANON

LAKE HULEH

Acre

Safed

SYRIA

Tiberias

LAKE TIBERIAS

Haifa   GALILEE

Nazareth

Beisan

Tulkarm

Qalqilyah

Jaffa Tel Aviv

Lydda

Ramallah

Ramleh

Latrun

Jerusalem and Bethlehem

TRANSJORDAN

DEAD SEA

Gaza

Beersheba

NEGEV

EGYPT

Aqaba

repulsed. Arab public opinion reacted with horror and alarm to these events.

On April 10 the Palestine Committee, a high-level political coordinating body set up by the Arab League, met to consider the three disasters that had just occurred: the death of Abd al-Qadir and the subsequent fall of Castel, the massacre at Deir Yassin, and Qawukji's defeat at Mishmar Haemek. For the first time, the assembled leaders gave serious consideration to the need for intervention by their regular army units in the wake of the failure of the Palestinian and ALA irregulars. But many more disasters were to follow before the Arab leaders would take their courage in their hands.

On April 18, in spite of their insistence on being the de jure authority in the country until the end of the Mandate, the British suddenly announced their withdrawal from Tiberias. This retreat paved the way for the conquest of Tiberias on the same day by the Haganah, and Tiberias became the first town to fall under Haganah control. Thousands of refugees streamed in panic into exile in Transjordan and Syria, creating a wave of shock and anger throughout the Arab world. Then on April 21 the British announced their withdrawal from Haifa; the Haganah promptly launched Operation Misparayim for the conquest of that city, which fell on April 22–23. Haifa was the first of the three major Palestinian cities (the other two being Jaffa and Jerusalem) to be conquered by the Haganah. Many more thousands of panic-stricken refugees fled either by sea to Lebanon and Egypt or overland across the Lebanese border.

During the last week of April, three other major operations were launched within the framework of Plan Dalet in different parts of the country: (1) Operation Chametz (April 25) to isolate and conquer Jaffa and the surrounding villages; (2) Operation Jevussi (April 26) to conquer the Palestinian residential quarters in West and East Jerusalem outside the Old City, as well as the villages in the northern and eastern suburbs; and (3) Operation Yiftach (April 28) to conquer the whole of eastern Galilee.

The Irgun anticipated Operation Chametz by launching its own offensive against Jaffa. By the end of April, the combined Haganah-Irgun offensives had completely encircled Jaffa, forcing most of the remaining civilians to flee by sea to Gaza or Egypt; many drowned in the process. A desperate attempt at resistance by a Palestinian ALA unit that penetrated into Jaffa was unsuccessful.

Operation Jevussi achieved its objectives within the city limits of West and East Jerusalem. The Palestinian residential quarters of Katamon, Talbiyya, the German Colony, the Greek Colony, Upper Bak'a, and Lower Bak'a, all in West Jerusalem, were conquered. Their inhabitants were driven into exile in Ramallah and Bethlehem, or across the Transjordanian border. The British, as the de jure authority, continued to hold certain enclaves in Jerusalem and to fly the Union Jack over the official residence of the high commissioner on the hill just south of the city, historically and appositely known as the Hill of Evil Counsel. Operation Jevussi was unsuccessful in the suburban villages to the north (Nabi Samu'il) and east (Tur), where Palestinian and ALA irregulars put up a stout resistance.

Operation Yiftach opened its first phase with the conquest of villages in the neighborhood of the Galilean town of Safed.

The pattern of attack in all three operations was the same: intensive, indiscriminate bombardment with mortars, of which the Haganah had an abundant supply, followed by coordinated attacks using infantry and armored cars. Great reliance was placed on simultaneous psychological warfare. The Palestinian collapse resulted from bad leadership, totally inadequate civil defense arrangements, and military disparity in planning, numbers, and firepower. By the end of April the Palestinian community was badly mangled. Tens of thousands of refugees were on the trek overland, with thousands more in transit at sea. The Arab governments could no longer ignore the pressure of public opinion on them to send their regular armies to help the Palestinians.

On April 30 Arab League leaders held a meeting in Amman, to which they summoned the chiefs of staff of their armies for counsel regarding the turn of events in Palestine. This was the very first such meeting of the Arab military heads. Accurately assessing Zionist strength, they estimated that the minimum force required to overcome the Haganah would be six divisions and six air squadrons. The political leaders, however, were unable or unwilling to bring themselves to believe this appraisal. Evidently, they still preferred to hope for a last-minute intervention by the Western powers, and to think that a mere show of force by their regular armies would bring it about. Therefore, they regarded the assessment of their military experts as exaggerated and unwarranted. They still could not contemplate intervention by the Arab armies before the formal end of the Mandate on May 15. And when the time for intervention came, a force less than half the minimum considered necessary by the military heads was all that was sent.

Meanwhile, the Haganah command pressed on with the business of Plan Dalet. On May 8–9 Operation Maccabi was launched to occupy and destroy the remaining villages in the central plain between Ramleh and Latrun. On May 11–12 the town of Safed was conquered; its inhabitants fled to Syria and Lebanon. The town of Beisan met the same fate on May 12; its inhabitants fled to Transjordan and Syria. On the same day Operation Barak was launched in the south to occupy and destroy the villages leading to the Negev. The inhabitants of these villages were driven into the Hebron hills.

Not until May 12 did Egypt, the strongest Arab country, agree to military intervention. Finally, its prime minister, bowing to Muslim and Arab public opinion, secured parliamentary approval for Egypt's intervention. The other Arab countries that had already agreed to intervene were Iraq, Syria, Lebanon, and Transjordan.

But the Arab countries' decision to intervene came too late if it was meant to prevent the destruction of the Palestinian community. It was also too late to prevent the establishment of the Jewish state.

On May 13 Chaim Weizmann wrote President Truman a letter asking for recognition of the Jewish state. On May 14 the British high commissioner left his official residence in Jerusalem on his way home to peaceful retirement in England. The new state came into existence at one minute after midnight Palestine time, or 6:01 P.M. Washington time. By 6:11 P.M. President Truman had recognized Israel.

Thus were sown the seeds of the Palestinian diaspora and the Arab-Israeli conflict.

CHRONOLOGY

1947 November 10: U.S. and Soviet Union agree to support UNSCOP partition plan, which calls for end to British Mandate by May 1.

November 29: UN General Assembly recommends slight variant of UNSCOP partition plan by 33 to 13 votes with 10 abstentions. Arab representatives walk out of Assembly.

November 30: Haganah calls up all Jews in Palestine aged 17 to 25 to register for military service.

December: Haganah emissaries in Czechoslovakia reach agreement with Skoda arms firm on supply of arms.

Haganah launches Plan Gimmel, designed to destabilize Palestinian population and occupy strategic positions in country.

December 2: Palestinians begin three-day strike protesting UN partition resolution. Intercommunal clashes result in death of eight Jews and six Palestinians.

December 5: U.S. State Department announces U.S. embargo on arms shipments to Palestine and the Arab states.

December 6: Irgun attacks Jaffa suburb of Abu Kebir.

December 8: Britain recommends to UN termination of Palestine Mandate on 15 May 1948 followed by creation of independent Jewish and Palestinian states two weeks later.

December 8–17: Arab League, meeting in Cairo, declares partition of Palestine illegal; it decides to put at disposal of Technical Military Committee 10,000 rifles, 3,000 volunteers (including 500 Palestinians), and additional £1,000,000.

December 13: Irgun carries out five raids on Palestinian residential areas in Jerusalem, Jaffa, and village of Tireh (Haifa district), killing 35 Palestinian civilians and wounding many others.

December 15: British turn policing of Tel Aviv and Petah Tikva over to Jews, and that of Jaffa over to Palestinians.

December 17: Jewish Agency Executive reports American Jews will be asked for $250 million to meet needs of Jewish community in Palestine.

December 19: Haganah attacks village of Khisas (Safed district), killing ten Palestinians.

December 20: Haganah attacks village of Qazaza (Ramleh district).

December 28: Irgun announces negotiations for "united front" with Haganah.

December 29: Irgunist grenade attack on Palestinian crowd at Herod's Gate in Jerusalem kills 17 civilians.

December 30: Irgunist grenade attack on Palestinian workers at Haifa refinery kills 6 and wounds 42. In reprisal, workers kill 41 Jewish refinery workers. In retaliation for reprisal, Haganah attacks village of Balad al-Sheikh, near Haifa, killing 17 Palestinians and injuring 33.

1948 January: British sell 20 Auster planes to Jewish authorities in Palestine.

British disband 3,200-strong Transjordanian Frontier Force (TJFF), recruited mainly from among Palestinians.

Abd al-Qadir al-Husseini, Palestinian guerrilla commander, secretly returns to Jerusalem after ten-year exile to organize resistance to partition.

January 1: Technical Military Committee of Arab League organizes volunteer force of Arab irregulars called Arab Liberation Army (ALA), under command of guerrilla leader Fawzi al-Qawukji, to help Palestinians resist partition.

January 3: Estimated 65,000 pounds of TNT destined for Haganah found being loaded aboard Palestine-bound freighter at Jersey City pier.

Haganah attacks village of Abu Shusha (Haifa district).

January 4: Irgun uses car bomb to blow up Grand Serai (government center) in Jaffa, killing 26 Palestinian civilians.

January 5: Haganah blows up Semiramis Hotel in Palestinian residential quarter of Jerusalem, killing 20 civilians.

January 7: Irgun plants explosives at Jaffa Gate in Jerusalem, killing 25 Palestinian civilians and wounding dozens.

January 8: First contingent of 330 ALA volunteers arrives in northern Palestine.

January 9: British troops clash with ALA volunteers attacking colonies of Dan and Kfar Szold.

January 14: Haganah emissaries conclude Czech Arms Deal. Payments total $12,280,000. Arms purchased include 24,500 rifles, 5,000 light machine guns, 200 medium machine guns, 54 million rounds of ammunition, and 25 Messerschmitts. Before end of Mandate, at least 10,740 rifles, 1,200 machine guns, 26 field guns, and 11 million rounds of ammunition arrive in Palestine. Balance of arms, including 25 Messerschmitts, arrives by end of May.

Palestinians plant bomb in Haifa post office, killing 6 Jews.

January 16: British report to UN estimates 1,974 persons killed or injured in Palestine between November 30 and January 10.

January 19: Haganah attacks villages of Shafa Amr and Tamra (Haifa and Nazareth districts, respectively).

January 20: Palestinian and ALA irregulars attack colony of Yehyam; British troops come to aid of colony.

January 21: Second contingent of 360 ALA volunteers arrives in Palestine.

January 26: Haganah destroys village of Sukreir (Gaza district).

January 28: Third contingent of 400 ALA volunteers arrives in Palestine.

February: Haganah office set up in U.S. under name "Land and Labor" for recruitment of professional military personnel (MAHAL).

February 1: Explosion caused by Palestinians at *Palestine Post* offices in Jerusalem kills 20 Jewish civilians.

February 6: Attack by ALA contingent on colony of Ein Zeitim broken up by British troops.

February 10: British troops repulse Palestinian irregulars attacking Jewish Montefiore quarter in Jerusalem.

February 14: Ben-Gurion issues orders to Haganah commander in Jerusalem for conquest of whole city and its suburbs.

Haganah attacks village of Sa'Sa (Safed district) and blows up 14 houses, killing 11 Palestinians.

February 15: Colony of Tirat Zvi in Jordan Valley repulses attack by ALA unit.

February 18: Haganah calls up men and women aged 25 to 35 for military service.

February 19: Three Jews killed when Haganah convoy ambushed near Manara (Tiberias district); British rescue convoy.

February 20: Ship *Independence* arrives at Tel Aviv with 280 volunteers under oath to Haganah on board, implementing policy of illegal immigration of military personnel.

Haganah shells Arab residential sections of Haifa with mortars, killing 6 and wounding 36 Palestinian civilians.

February 22: Palestinian irregulars blow up buildings on Ben Yehuda Street in Jerusalem, killing 57 Jewish civilians and injuring 100.

February 24: U.S. delegate to UN says role of Security Council regarding Palestine to keep peace, not enforce partition. Syrian delegate proposes appointment of committee to explore possibility of Jewish Agency–Arab Higher Committee agreement.

February 27: Jewish Agency announces it will establish state even without backing of an international force.

March 2: U.S. delegate tells Security Council U.S. favors implementing partition by "peaceful measures" only.

March 3: Stern Gang destroys office building in Haifa with car bomb, killing 11 and injuring 27 Palestinian civilians.

March 5–7: Fawzi al-Qawukji enters Palestine and assumes command of ALA units in central Palestine.

March 5: Two ALA units, of 360 volunteers each, enter Jaffa to aid resistance.

Haganah attacks and captures village of Biyar Adas (Jaffa district), expelling its inhabitants.

March 6: Haganah declares general mobilization and defends its right to mobilize any Jews of military age resident in Palestine, including American citizens.

March 10: British House of Commons votes to terminate Mandate as of May 15.

Plan Dalet finalized by Haganah.

March 11: Palestinians blow up Jewish Agency headquarters in Jerusalem, killing 12 and injuring 86 Jewish civilians.

March 12: Haganah blows up houses in Jaffa suburb of Abu Kebir.

March 13: Haganah blows up houses in village of Huseiniyeh (Safed district).

March 16: Palestinian irregulars block road to Zionist colonies in Negev at village of Bureir (Gaza district).

March 17: Haganah ambushes Palestinian convoy en route to Haifa, killing Arab commander of Haifa garrison.

March 18: Palestinian irregulars ambush Haganah convoy at village of Artuf near Latrun, west of Jerusalem, killing 11 Haganah members.

President Truman secretly receives Chaim Weizmann at White House, and pledges support for declaration of Jewish state on May 15.

March 19: Ben-Gurion declares Jewish state dependent not on UN partition decision, but on Jewish military preponderance.

U.S. delegate asks Security Council to suspend action on partition plan, and to call special session of General Assembly to work on trusteeship solution.

March 20: Arab League announces Arab acceptance of truce and limited trusteeship for Palestine if Jews agree to same; Jewish Agency rejects Palestine trusteeship.

March 21: Palestinian irregulars explode car bomb on Harbour Street in Haifa, causing 20 Jewish casualties.

March 22: Car bomb left by Jews dressed in British army uniforms explodes on Iraq Street in Haifa, causing 23 Palestinian casualties.

Haganah destroys village of Jebalya, near Jaffa.

March 24: Haganah destroys Bedouin hamlets near Yevniel, west of Tiberias.

Colony of Atarot, north of Jerusalem, attacked by Palestinian irregulars.

March 25: President Truman calls for immediate Arab-Jewish truce and says U.S. will share responsibility for temporary trusteeship.

March 26: Palestine Post Office Department suspends all mail service to Palestine except airmail letters.

March 27: Palestinian and ALA irregulars ambush Haganah convoy en route to Yehyam in western Galilee, killing 45 Haganah members; British troops come to aid of convoy.

Palestinian irregulars ambush Haganah convoy en route to Gush Etzion, near Hebron, killing 70 Haganah members; British troops intervene to arrange surrender of others at Neve Daniel, south of Bethlehem.

March 28: Thirteen half-tracks (out of consignment of 50) reach Haganah from U.S.

March 30: U.S. delegate presents resolution to Security Council calling for truce to be arranged with Jewish Agency and Arab Higher Committee representatives.

March 31: Haganah completes demolition of Abu Kebir, village near Jaffa.

Zionist assailants blow up train near colony of Benjamina, killing 24 Palestinians and injuring 61.

Palestinian irregulars ambush Haganah convoy at village of Hulda, east of Ramleh.

April 1: Security Council votes to call special session of General Assembly, and agrees to U.S. truce proposal of March 30.

Ship *Nora*, carrying 4,500 rifles, 200 light machine guns, and 5 million rounds of ammunition, arrives in Haifa from Split, Yugoslavia. In tandem, 200 rifles, 40 machine guns, and more ammunition arrive by plane at secret Haganah airfield. Both consignments constitute first installment of Czech Arms Deal (see January 14, May 12–14).

April 2: Haganah attacks and captures Palestinian village of Castel, west of Jerusalem, expelling its inhabitants.

April 4: Haganah launches Plan Dalet.

Qawukji attacks Zionist colony of Mishmar Haemek, southeast of Haifa.

April 5: Palestinian and Zionist leaders object to U.S. proposals presented to Security Council for temporary trusteeship agreement.

Haganah launches Operation Nachshon (first phase of Plan Dalet); villages of Hulda and Deir Muheisin, east of Ramleh, attacked and captured.

April 5–6: Qawukji agrees to 24-hour cease-fire at Mishmar Haemek at request of colony's inhabitants and British; Haganah breaks cease-fire.

Palestinian counterattack at Hulda and Deir Muheisin fails.

April 8: Haganah starts offensive against Palestinian town of Tiberias.

April 9: Abd al-Qadir al-Husseini killed in counterattack at Castel; Haganah retakes Castel.

Haganah attacks and occupies villages of Ji'ara, Kafrin, Abu Zureiq, and Abu Shusha, southeast of Haifa.

Irgun and Stern Gang massacre some 245 inhabitants in village of Deir Yassin, western suburb of Jerusalem three miles from Castel.

April 10: In wake of Deir Yassin massacre and failure of Palestinian and ALA irregulars, special Palestine Committee set up by Arab League meets to discuss security situation in Palestine.

Zionist colony of Kfar Darom in Negev attacked by unit of irregulars organized by Egyptian Muslim Brotherhood.

April 11: Haganah destroys village of Kolonia, near Castel, and occupies Deir Yassin.

April 12: General Zionist Council resolves to establish independent Jewish state in Palestine on May 16.

Haganah, Irgun, and Stern Gang negotiate agreement for joint operations.

Zionist colonists from Gush Etzion ambush traffic on Hebron-Jerusalem road. Transjordanian Arab Legion units, operating in Palestine under British command, shell Gush Etzion in retaliation.

April 13–20: At conclusion of Operation Nachshon, Haganah launches Operation Harel; villages of Biddu, Beit Surik, Saris, and Suba (Jerusalem district) attacked and destroyed.

April 13: Qawukji withdraws from Mishmar Haemek; Haganah attacks and occupies neighboring villages of Naghnaghiya, Mansi, and Lajjun.

Palestinian irregulars ambush Haganah-escorted convoy en route to Hebrew University in East Jerusalem; 39 Jews and 6 Palestinians killed.

April 14: Security Council resolution calls for military and political truce.

Haganah attacks Palestinian Druze villages of Hosha and Khirbet Qasir, near Haifa.

April 16: Counterattack by Druze irregulars forces Haganah to withdraw from Hosha.

British evacuate town of Safed.

April 18: In wake of sudden British withdrawal from Tiberias, Haganah attacks and captures town; Palestinian inhabitants flee.

Haganah starts offensive against town of Safed.

April 20: U.S. submits trusteeship plan for Palestine to UN.

Palestinians block coastal road to Jewish quarters of Jerusalem; fierce battle ensues to intercept Haganah convoy near village of Deir Ayyub, west of Jerusalem.

April 21: British suddenly evacuate residential quarters of Haifa.

April 22: Haganah launches Operation Misparayim to attack and occupy Haifa.

April 23: Villages of Beit Iksa and Shu'fat, north of Jerusalem, attacked and captured by Haganah, but Haganah repulsed at Nabi Sam'uil.

Haganah captures Haifa; Palestinian inhabitants flee.

April 24: Irgun starts offensive against Jaffa with heavy mortar shelling followed by infantry attack.

April 25–31: Launching Operation Chametz to conquer Jaffa, Haganah attacks suburban villages of Tell Rish, Yazur, and Salameh.

April 25: Twenty-five artillery pieces on board *Resurrectio* reach Tel Aviv.

April 26: Launching Operation Jevussi for conquest of whole of Jerusalem, Haganah attacks Palestinian residential quarter of Sheikh Jarrah in East Jerusalem, cutting off city from north; British forces intervene against Haganah.

Haganah's attempt at cutting off Jerusalem from Jericho fails.

April 27: Haganah announces coordination of plans with Irgun.

April 28–30: Palestinian ALA unit under Michel Issa succeeds in fighting its way into Jaffa in order to break Haganah siege.

April 28: British intervene to stop joint Irgun-Haganah attack against Jaffa.

Haganah launches Operation Matate to expel Palestinians of eastern Galilee (from Rosh Pina to Jordan River).

Haganah launches Operation Yiftach to expel Palestinians from rest of eastern and central Galilee, and to capture Safed.

Haganah attacks Palestinian town of Samakh, south of Lake Tiberias; inhabitants flee city.

Haganah attacks and occupies villages of Ein Zeitun and Biriya, north of Safed.

April 29: Haganah captures Jaffa suburbs of Salameh, Yazur, and Jebalya, cutting off Jaffa from hinterland; remaining residents flee city by sea, but ALA relief units and other volunteers maintain resistance.

Continuing Operation Jevussi, Haganah attacks and occupies Palestinian residential quarter of Katamon in West Jerusalem.

April 30: All Palestinian quarters in West Jerusalem occupied by Haganah, and residents driven out.

First meeting of chiefs of staff of Arab armies to review situation in Palestine held in Amman.

May 1: Lebanon and Syria decide to send troops to Palestine at end of Mandate on May 15.

May 2: Iraq dispatches troops to town of Mafraq, in Transjordan, en route to Palestine after May 15.

Three planeloads of arms for Haganah arrive from France.

May 3: Between 175,000 and 200,000 Palestinian refugees reported to have fled east from Zionist-occupied areas.

Jewish colonists from Gush Etzion, south of Jerusalem, ambush traffic on road to city.

May 4: Unit of Transjordanian Arab Legion, operating in Palestine under British command, shells Gush Etzion in retaliation for ambush.

Irgun units occupy village of Abbasiyah, near Jaffa.

Britain announces it is studying transitional trusteeship regime for Palestine to take effect at end of Mandate.

May 5: ALA unit under Michel Issa withdraws from Jaffa, ending city's resistance.

May 6: Five artillery pieces reach Haganah from France.

Haganah attacks and occupies village of Shejara and neighboring villages around Mt. Tabor; inhabitants driven out.

Haganah offensive to occupy Safed intensifies.

May 8–9: Haganah launches Operation Maccabi for conquest of remaining villages between Ramleh and Latrun; village of Beit Mahsir, west of Latrun, attacked.

May 10–12: Arab chiefs of staff meet in Damascus.

May 10: Haganah enters Jaffa.

Kfar Darom, colony in Negev, again attacked by Egyptian irregular units.

May 11: Continuing Operation Maccabi, Haganah occupies village of Beit Muheisir, west of Latrun.

Haganah launches Operation Gideon to occupy villages in Huleh basin, upper eastern Galilee.

May 11–12: Haganah captures Safed and surrounding villages.

May 12–14: Second and third airlifts of arms from Communist-controlled Czechoslovakia arrive in Palestine for Haganah, delivering 5,000 rifles, 1,200 machine guns, and 6 million rounds of ammunition.

May 12: State of emergency declared in all Arab countries, and able-bodied Palestinian men barred entry to them.

Egyptian Parliament decides to send troops to Palestine at end of Mandate.

Unit of Transjordanian Arab Legion presses attack against Gush Etzion.

At Latrun, Palestinian irregulars again block road from coast to Jewish quarters of Jerusalem.

Haganah launches Operation Barak to occupy villages of Bureir, Huleikat, and Kawkabah, as well as neighboring villages (Gaza district); operation intended to "open the way" to the Negev.

Continuing Operation Gideon, Haganah occupies' villages of Ulam, Hadatha, and Ma'dhar (Tiberias district, lower Galilee); "area now empty of Arabs," according to Haganah sources.

Haganah attacks and occupies town of Beisan, south of Lake Tiberias.

May 13: Chaim Weizmann sends President Truman letter requesting U.S. recognition of Jewish state upon its proclamation.

UN appoints Count Folke Bernadotte as mediator to resolve conflict in Palestine.

Fifty artillery pieces and 24 heavy mortars arrive for Haganah at Haifa on board *Borea*.

Irgun-Haganah agreement signed for conquest of whole of Jerusalem.

Unit of Transjordanian Arab Legion and Palestinian irregulars capture Kfar Etzion, one of four colonies comprising Gush Etzion (*gush* = "bloc").

Jaffa leaders sign document of surrender to Haganah.

Haganah attacks and occupies villages of Aqir, Katra, Bashit, Beit Daras, and Barqah (Ramleh district).

Haganah ordered to occupy all Palestinian villages in coastal plain near Tulkarm.

Village of Tireh, near town of Qalqilyah, repulses Haganah attack.

Haganah attacks Palestinian hamlets on slopes of Mt. Carmel, occupies village of Kafr Saba, and starts abortive offensive to capture Qalqilyah.

May 14: Haganah launches Operation Klashon to occupy strategic areas in Jerusalem evacuated by British and Palestinian residential quarters outside Old City.

Haganah launches Operation Schfifon for capture of Old City of Jerusalem.

Haganah launches Operation Ben Ami for conquest of upper western Galilee; villages of Sumeiriya, Zeeb, and Bassa (Acre district) attacked and occupied.

Villages of Kafr Qar'a (Haifa district), Qubab (Lydda district), and Abu Shusha (Jaffa district) captured by Haganah.

Three remaining colonies of Gush Etzion (Revadim, Ein Tsurim, and Massuor Yitzhak), south of Jerusalem, surrender to unit of Transjordanian Arab Legion.

British high commissioner leaves residence in Jerusalem en route to Britain.

State of Israel proclaimed in Tel Aviv at 4:00 P.M.

May 15: British Mandate ends.

Declaration of state of Israel comes into effect.

President Truman recognizes state of Israel.

First Egyptian regular troops cross border into Palestine.

Egyptian troops attack colonies of Kfar Darom and Nirim in Negev.

Three Transjordanian Arab Legion brigades cross Jordan River into Palestine.

Lebanese regulars retake Lebanese villages of Malkiya and Qadas (on Lebanese border), attacked and captured earlier by Haganah.

Zionist colonies of Atarot and Neve Yaqov, north of Jerusalem, as well as colony near Jericho, evacuated by Haganah.

May 16: Syrian column advances toward Palestinian town of Samakh, south of Lake Tiberias, attacked and occupied earlier by Haganah.

Continuing Operation Ben Ami, Haganah attacks city of Acre.

Arab Legion units reach northern suburbs of Jerusalem.

May 17: Haganah continues Operation Schfifon for conquest of Old City of Jerusalem.

Haganah captures Acre.

May 18: Syrian troops retake Samakh and capture Zionist colonies of Shaar Hagolan and Masada.

Arab Legion units reach Latrun and consolidate blockade of coastal road to Jewish quarters in Jerusalem.

May 19: Egyptian troops attack colony of Yad Mordechai in Negev.

Haganah breaks into Old City of Jerusalem.

Arab Legion comes to rescue of Old City.

Political Developments

The British Entrapped

387 Barbed wire and other barriers put up by the British around their administrative compound (left) in central Jerusalem, for protection against acts of terrorism by Zionist groups, fall 1947.

The Importation of a Military Industry

388 As early as 1945, David Ben-Gurion (then chairman of the Jewish Agency Executive) arranged on a visit to the United States for the purchase of entire military plants, which were being sold ostensibly as scrap at the end of the war. The machinery was smuggled to Palestine during the British Mandate, and secretly installed in heavily populated Jewish neighborhoods (see 303–304). This photograph shows a plant for the production of armored cars, mid-1948.

388

387

389

Partition at the United Nations

389 On 29 November 1947 a resolution recommending the partition of Palestine into a Jewish state and a Palestinian state was virtually forced through the United Nations General Assembly by the United States. It was received with shock and consternation by the entire Arab and Muslim worlds. Here a vast crowd in Cairo protests the resolution, December 1947.

390 The UN partition recommendation (a resolution by the UN General Assembly is not binding) precipitated a series of Jewish-Palestinian clashes. These clashes escalated into total civil war during the remaining months of the British Mandate, which ended on 15 May 1948. The Palestinians were determined not to accept the establishment of a Zionist state on their soil nor to become a minority under foreign rule in such a state; the Zionists were equally determined to establish a Zionist state with or without Palestinian consent. An early incident (shown here) was the burning of the Palestinian-owned Rex Cinema on the border between the Jewish and Palestinian halves of Jerusalem in December 1947.

Zionist Terrorism

391 A bomb thrown from a passing taxi at a bus in the Palestinian residential quarter outside Herod's Gate, Jerusalem, on 29 December 1947 killed seventeen Palestinian civilians. The perpetrators were members of the Irgun (see 294–295). This was one of hundreds of such attacks by Zionist terrorist groups that occurred in the subsequent months.

390

391

392

392 Palestinian policeman carrying a child victim of the incident recorded in 391.

393 Ruins of the Grand Serai, Jaffa (see 6, 164). A truck loaded with explosives covered with oranges was parked outside the entrance on 4 January 1948 by members of the Stern Gang (see 293). The resulting explosion destroyed the building and killed twenty-six Palestinian civilians.

394 Ruins of the Semiramis Hotel, located in the Palestinian residential quarter of Bak'a in West Jerusalem. On 5 January 1948 (the day after the incident recorded in 393) members of the Haganah blew up the hotel, killing twenty civilian guests including women and children (see 308).

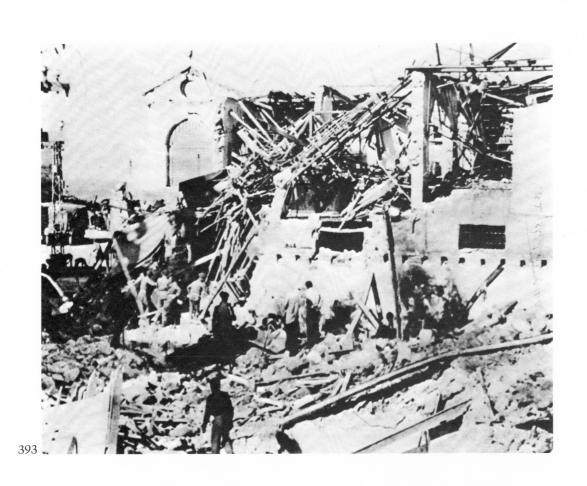

393

394

395

396

395 Palestinian civilians (and British constables) taking cover from sniper fire, Jerusalem, February 1948.

Palestinian Resistance and Retaliation

396 Early in January 1948 Abd al-Qadir al-Husseini (see 78, 253, 409–411) returned to Palestine after an exile of ten years, and began organizing Palestinian resistance to the forcible partition of Palestine. He is seen here (standing center) with aides and Palestinian irregulars, Jerusalem district, February 1948.

397–399 Members of the Palestinian resistance, 1948.

397

398

399

400

400–402 Adopting the tactics introduced by Zionist terrorists, the Palestinian resistance struck back with booby-trapped vehicles against Jewish targets: (400) an explosion at the offices of the *Palestine Post* in Jerusalem killed twenty Jewish civilians on 1 February 1948; (401) fifty-seven Jewish civilians died in an explosion on Ben Yehuda Street in Jerusalem on 22 February 1948; (402) twelve Jewish civilians were killed at the Jewish Agency headquarters in Jerusalem on 11 March 1948.

401

402

Volunteers from Abroad Join Both Sides

403, 404 Both sides received volunteers from outside the country. The Zionists had two organizations for the purpose of recruiting such volunteers: GAHAL and MAHAL. GAHAL trained some twenty thousand volunteers at various European bases and transported them to Palestine. MAHAL secured the services of professional personnel and military experts. In the period before 15 May 1948, the Arab League sponsored the formation of an irregular force of about three thousand volunteers known as the Arab Liberation Army (ALA); about 2,500 of these volunteers came from neighboring Arab countries, and the rest were Palestinians. Returning to Palestine to assume command of ALA units in the central part of the country, Fawzi al-Qawukji (see 263–264) is seen in 403 on his arrival at the village of Jaba, near Nablus, in early March 1948. ALA irregulars are pictured in 404 in central Palestine, March 1948.

403

The Battle for the Roads

405–408 Nearly all of the Zionist colonies (see 296–298) belonged to a centrally directed Zionist military network. They were impregnable to the light arms possessed by the Palestinians, and posed a formidable threat to Palestinian communications. The Zionist leadership used the colonies both to disrupt Palestinian communications and to stake out territorial claims for a state extending beyond the frontiers of the Jewish state envisioned in the UN partition recommendation (see 389). The Palestinians countered by trying to block the passage of reinforcements to the colonies. Photographs 405, 406, and 407, taken in the Jerusalem district in the spring of 1948, show an armored truck carrying fortification materials, an armored personnel carrier, and an armored car with an armor-plated bus behind it. These vehicles — all captured by Palestinian irregulars — were typical of vehicles used to carry reinforcements to Zionist colonies. In 408, Palestinian irregulars deploy to set up an ambush, Hebron district, spring 1948.

406

405

407

408

Castel and Deir Yassin

The general offensive for the conquest of as much of Palestine as possible was launched by the Zionist leadership on 4 April 1948 within the framework of Plan Dalet (Hebrew for *D*), drawn up by the Haganah. One of its first objectives was to conquer the scores of Palestinian villages between Jaffa and Jerusalem through a series of coordinated military operations designated Nachshon, Harel, and Maccabi. All these villages lay outside the boundaries of the Jewish state envisioned in the UN partition recommendation (see 389).

On 2 April 1948, three days before Operation Nachshon commenced, the Haganah attacked and occupied the Palestinian village of Castel, about five miles west of Jerusalem, expelling its inhabitants.

409 On the night of April 7–8, under the command of Abd al-Qadir al-Husseini (see 253, 396), Palestinian irregulars counterattacked the Haganah occupiers of Castel. The Palestinians are seen here moving to the counterattack.

410 On April 9 the Palestinians recaptured Castel, but Abd al-Qadir was killed while leading his men. This is a photograph of his funeral at the Mosque of the Dome of the Rock in Jerusalem. (For the funeral of his father, Musa Kazim Pasha al-Husseini, see 111–112.)

409

410

411

411 While Abd al-Qadir was battling the Haganah at Castel on 9 April 1948, eighty men of the Irgun, on orders from Menachem Begin, attacked the tiny village of Deir Yassin (shown here) in the western suburbs of Jerusalem, about three miles east of Castel and next to the Jewish neighborhood of Givat Sha'ul. One month earlier, Deir Yassin had asked for and signed a nonaggression pact with Givat Sha'ul. Nevertheless, it was from Givat Sha'ul that the Irgun attackers emerged, together with forty armed men of the Stern Gang (one of whose three top leaders was Yitzhak Shamir, current prime minister of Israel). "The attackers perpetrated an indiscriminate massacre in the village, killing men and women, children and the elderly. They ended their operation by putting their 'prisoners' in trucks and touring the streets of the Jewish sector of Jerusalem in a 'victory parade.' The 'prisoners' were then returned to the village and killed. The number of villagers killed was 245, including men, women, and children."[1]

Altogether nearly two hundred Palestinian villages were attacked and conquered by Zionist forces before the end of the Mandate on 15 May 1948. Many of the inhabitants suffered injury or death, and all were expelled or fled in fear from their homes.

The Siege and Fall of Jaffa

In accordance with Plan Dalet, Haganah attacks were mounted against the major towns. Tiberias fell on April 18; Haifa, after fierce fighting, on April 23. On April 24, Menachem Begin opened an attack by the Irgun on the Manshiyeh quarter of Jaffa, a narrow Palestinian suburb located beside the sea and largely surrounded by Tel Aviv. Throughout four days and nights, under Begin's direction, the Irgun indiscriminately shelled the population of Jaffa with mortars — an early rehearsal for a later siege by Begin of an Arab city in 1982. Meanwhile, attacking from the west and south, the Haganah launched Operation Chametz in order to encircle Jaffa and cut it off from the rest of the country.

412 Ruins of the Manshiyeh quarter.

413 Irgunists moving through holes blasted in Palestinian houses.

414 With no proper military organization or civil defense, the morale of the Palestinian civilian population broke under the twin offensives by the Haganah and the Irgun. Here women and children salvage some belongings as they flee the city.

413

412

336

414

415

Into the Sea

415 Palestinians driven into the sea at Jaffa Harbor,
late April 1948. With the land routes cut off by
the Haganah, tens of thousands of the citizens of
Jaffa and neighboring villages fled by boat to
Gaza and Egypt; scores were drowned. Jaffa was
to have been the main port of the Palestinian
state envisioned in the UN partition recommendation of 29 November 1947 (see 389).

The Fall of Acre and the Conquest of Western Galilee

In accordance with Plan Dalet (see 409–411), the attacks on the main towns continued into May. On May 12 the town of Safed fell in Operation Yiftach. After the fall of Haifa, the Haganah launched Operation Ben Ami, aimed at conquering western Galilee and annexing it to the Jewish state. Western Galilee lay outside the boundaries of the Jewish state envisioned in the UN recommendation of 29 November 1947.

416 Haganah forces laying siege to Acre, ca. 16 May 1948. Acre also lay outside the Jewish state as envisioned in the UN partition recommendation.

417 Civilian inhabitants of Acre being herded into prison after the fall of the town, 17 May 1948.

418 Ruins of the village of Sumeiriya, just north of Acre, typifying the fate of nearly four hundred Palestinian villages by the end of 1948.

Tens of thousands of Palestinians who were expelled from the towns and villages of Galilee sought refuge across the border in Lebanon, where they constituted the core of the Palestinian refugee population in that country.[2]

417

416

418

Ben-Gurion and the Conquest of Jerusalem

As early as February 1948, David Ben-Gurion had drawn up a plan for the conquest of the whole of Jerusalem, including the Palestinian quarters, although the city and its environs were envisioned as a *corpus separatum* under a United Nations trusteeship according to the UN partition recommendation of 29 November 1947. Ben-Gurion's plan was divided into two phases. During Phase 1 (to be implemented until the end of the British Mandate on 15 May 1948), a principal objective was "to seize every military and political opportunity to control the residential quarters of the enemy in order to produce geographic Jewish contiguity throughout the city and to move Jews into these quarters as their inhabitants leave them." Phase 2 was to be implemented once the British left; its objective was "the liberation of the Old City and the whole of Jerusalem."[3]

Operation Jevussi was launched on April 26 to implement Phase 1. By April 30 most of the Palestinian quarters in West Jerusalem (see 327–328, 332) and some in East Jerusalem had been occupied and their inhabitants expelled. On 14 May 1948 Operation Klashon completed the work of Jevussi outside the Old City. On the same day Operation Schfifon was launched for the conquest of the Old City, which was all of Jerusalem that remained in Palestinian hands. Only the heroism of its defenders and the belated intervention, on 19 May 1948, of units of the Arab Legion of Transjordan prevented the fall of the Old City with the rest of East Jerusalem and their annexation by Ben-Gurion in 1948.

419

420

419 A Haganah military column arrives in Jerusalem from Tel Aviv, April 1948, in accordance with Plan Dalet (see 409–411).

420 Night fighting in Jerusalem, early May 1948.

421–423 Scenes of devastation in the Palestinian residential quarters of East Jerusalem, April to early May 1948: (421) ruins of a house in the Sa'ad-Sa'id quarter; (422) ruins of the Musrara quarter; (423) ruins of the commercial center outside Jaffa Gate. In 423, what was left of the Hotel Fast appears rear right, and the ruins on the far left side of the street are those of the Arab Bank's headquarters. (For street scenes in this area before the fighting, see, e.g. 207, 277.)

421

422

423

Count Bernadotte

424 On 13 May 1948 Count Folke Bernadotte, member of the Swedish royal family and International Red Cross representative in Europe during the later stages of World War II, was appointed by the United Nations as a mediator to seek a settlement of the Palestine conflict. On 17 September 1948 he was murdered in the Zionist-controlled section of Jerusalem. His assassins belonged to a "dissident" group that had allegedly broken away from the Stern Gang (see 293).

Abandoning Ship

425 General Sir Alan Cunningham, British high commissioner, inspecting a guard of honor as he left his official residence in Jerusalem for the last time, 14 May 1948. The British Mandate for Palestine came to its ignominious end on 15 May 1948. (See 16, 79)

425

424

The First Palestinian Diaspora

By 15 May 1948 hundreds of thousands of Palestinian refugees from scores of Palestinian towns and hundreds of Palestinian villages had been scattered to the four winds in the neighboring Arab countries. On 5 June 1948 David Ben-Gurion wrote in his diary: "We must make immediate preparations for settlement of the abandoned villages with the assistance of the Jewish National Fund."[4]

426 A typical Palestinian refugee camp at Nahr al-Barid in northern Lebanon, winter 1948.

427 "If Winter comes, can Spring be far behind?"

426

NOTES

Jerusalem: Allah's Choice

1. Quotation from a work by Burhan al-Din al-Fazari, lecturer and preacher at the Umayyad Mosque in Damascus, and leading Arab geographer of his time; he died in A.D. 1329.

Jesus: Allah's Word

1. Koran, sura 4, verse 171.

I. The Last Days of Ottoman Rule, 1876–1918

Introduction

1. Miguel Asin, *Islam and the Divine Comedy*, trans. and abridged Harold Sunderland (London: John Murray, 1926), pp. 67–76.

2. *Report by Sir William Fitzgerald on the Local Administration of Jerusalem* (Jerusalem: Government Printer, 1945), p. 4.

3. Quoted in A. L. Tibawi, "Jerusalem: Its Place in Islam and Arab History," *Arab World* 14, nos. 10–11 (1968): 11.

4. *Encyclopedia of Islam*, new ed., s.v. "Filastin."

5. Ibid.

6. Philip K. Hitti, *History of the Arabs from the Earliest Times to the Present*, 8th ed. (London: Macmillan & Co.; New York: St. Martin's Press, 1964), p. 439.

7. Tibawi, "Jerusalem," p. 11.

8. Stanley Lane-Poole, *Saladin and the Fall of the Kingdom of Jerusalem* (Beirut: Khayats, 1964), p. 234.

9. St. H. Stephan, "An Endowment Deed of Khasseki Sultan, Dated the 24th of May 1552," *Quarterly of the Department of Antiquities in Palestine*, vol. 10, no. 4, pp. 170–94.

10. Amnon Cohen, *Jewish Life under Islam: Jerusalem in the Sixteenth Century* (Cambridge, Mass. and London: Harvard University Press, 1984), p. 34.

Commentary

1. Félix Bonfils (1831–85) and his son Adrien (1860–1929) were among the first European photographers to live and work in the Middle East. The photographs of Félix date from 1867 to ca. 1877, those of Adrien from 1877 to ca. 1895. Photographs presented in Part I that are known to be by "Bonfils" are identified as such in their respective captions.

II. From the British Occupation to the Great Palestine Rebellion, 1918–1935

Introduction

1. See the testimony of Rabbi Stephen S. Wise in *Admission of German Refugee Children, Joint Hearings on S.J. Res. 64 and H.J. Res. 168*, 76th Cong., 1st sess., 1939, pp. 155–60. See also Robert Briscoe with Alden Hatch, *For the Life of Me* (Boston: Little, Brown & Co., 1958), pp. 266–70.

Commentary

1. *A Survey of Palestine: Prepared in December 1945 and January 1946 for the Information of the Anglo-American Committee of Inquiry*, 2 vols. and supp. (Jerusalem: Government of Palestine, 1946), 1:323.

2. *The Area of Cultivable Land in Palestine* (Jerusalem: Jewish Agency, 1936), p. 13.

3. *Survey of Palestine*, 1:314–39.

4. *Survey of Palestine*, 1:331.

5. U.S. Government, *Documents of the Jerusalem Consulate*, Gillman to Porter, 16 December 1886.

6. *Survey of Palestine*, 1:339.

III. The Great Rebellion, 1936–1939

Commentary

1. *Survey of Palestine*, 1:38.

2. David Ben-Gurion, *Jewish Observer and Middle East Review*, 20 September 1963, pp. 13–14.

3. *Survey of Palestine*, 2:594–95.

4. Leonard Mosley, *Gideon Goes to War* (New York: Scribner, 1955), pp. 63–64.

5. *Survey of Palestine*, 1:43, 46, 49.

IV. From the London Conference to the UN Partition Recommendation, 1939–1947

Introduction

1. See the Introduction to Part II, p. 87.

2. Nicholas Bethell, *The Palestine Triangle: The Struggle between the British, the Jews, and the Arabs, 1935–48* (London: André Deutsch, 1979), p. 347. The figures are for the period from August 1945 to September 1947.

IV. *continued*

Commentary

1. For Shamir's views on the permissibility of political assassination, see Bethell, *The Palestine Triangle,* pp. 277–78.

2. The Haganah was official in the sense that it was under the direct command of the Zionist leadership in the Jewish Agency. The British did not officially recognize it, but turned a blind eye to its existence.

V. Civil War and the Destruction of the Palestinian Community, November 1947–May 1948

Introduction

1. Evan M. Wilson, *Decision on Palestine* (Stanford, Calif.: Hoover Institution Press, 1979), p. 127.

2. "Reflections on Zionist Policy," *The Jewish Frontier* (October 1948): 7–11.

3. P. J. Loftus, *National Income of Palestine, 1944* (Jerusalem: Government Printer, 1946), p. 48.

4. Head of Command, Jewish Resistance Movement, to Joint Chairman [*sic*], Anglo-American Committee of Inquiry, 25 March 1946, Jerusalem, p. 11.

5. Moshe Pearlman, *Ben-Gurion Looks Back in Talks with Moshe Pearlman* (New York: Simon & Schuster, 1965), pp. 138–39.

6. Benzion Dinur, ed., *Sefer Toldot Ha-Haganah* ["The Official History of the Haganah," unpublished in English], 8 vols. (Tel Aviv: Zionist Library — Marakhot, 1954–72), 3:1253–55, appendix 39:1939–43.

7. Ibid., 3:1472–75, appendix 48:1955–60.

8. See the Introduction to Part IV, p. 238.

9. Harry S. Truman, *Years of Trial and Hope* (London: Hodder and Stoughton; New York: Doubleday, 1956), 2:161.

10. M. W. Weisgal and S. Carmichael, eds., *Chaim Weizmann: A Biography by Several Hands* (London: Weidenfeld & Nicolson, 1962), pp. 303–8.

Commentary

1. Dinur, ed., *Toldot Ha-Haganah,* vol. 3, chap. 77, pp. 1546ff.

2. See Nafez Nazzal, *The Palestinian Exodus from Galilee, 1948* (Beirut: Institute for Palestine Studies, 1978).

3. Dinur, ed., *Toldot Ha-Haganah,* chap. 70, pp. 1395ff.

4. David Ben-Gurion, *A Personal History of Israel* (New York: Funk & Wagnalls; New York — Tel Aviv: Sabra Books, 1971), p. 123. The Jewish National Fund (Keren Kayemeth) was founded in 1901; see the Chronology for Part I, p. 38.

PHOTOGRAPHIC CREDITS

Key to Letters Prefacing Catalogue Numbers

H: Haj Amin al-Husseini collection
J: Wasif Jawhariyyah collection
R: Khalil Raad collection
WK: Walid Khalidi, personal collection
PC: Institute for Palestine Studies, Photograph
   Collection
PLO: Palestine Liberation Organization
   Information Center archives
Q or E: Imperial War Museum collection
M: Matson Photo Service, Library of Congress

No. 1. R-453
2. R-1957
3. J1/12
3a. WK1
3b. WK2
4. J1/37
5. R-671
6. J1/44
7. J1/20
8. R-933
9. R-922
10. Q59305
11. Q12301
12. Q52135
13. Q82517
14. Q13213
15. J2/7
16. Q55530
17. Q12331
18. Q12325
19. Q12335
20. R-296
21. R-308
22. R-309
23. R-154
24. R-1978
25. PC81/46
26. PC81/64
27. R-160
28. PC81/63
29. R-2507
30. PC81/240
31. J6/45

No. 32. J6/39
33. J6/43
34. PC81/39
35. R-96
36. R-167
37. PC81/43
38. R-715
39. PC81/56
40. PC81/47
41. PC81/48
42. M36-313
43. PC81/44
44. PC81/45
45. J7/32
46. R-297
47. R-432
48. R-168
49. PC81/52
50. R-960
51. PC81/51
52. R-48
53. R-147
54. PC81/42
55. R-220
56. J7/30
57. PC81/65
58. R-3
59. PC81/84
60. PC81/140
61. J5/19(206)
62. PC81/32
63. PC81/83
64. PC81/87

No. 65. PC81/31
66. J5/18
67. J1/15
68. J1/17
69. PC81/264
70. J5/17
71. J5/1(156)
72. R-91
73. J1/61
74. J5/11
75. J1/50
76. J1/31
77. PC81/37
78. J4/7
79. J2/23
80. J2/19(50)
81. J2/19(49)
82. PC81/77
83. PC81/78
84. J2/41
85. PC81/112
86. H-20
86a. PC81/331
86b. PC81/335
87. PC81/79
88. H-34
89. J4/35
90. R-1338
91. M33-4138
92. J2/59
93. M33-4151
94. J2/61
95. M32-4146
96. R-1315
97. R-1314
98. J3/17
99. J3/25
100. J3/7
101. PC81/169
102. PC81/118
103. J3/14
104. PC81/173
105. PC81/321
106. J3/35
107. M33-4210
108. M33-4216

No. 109. M33-4212
110. J3/32
111. PC81/144
112. PC81/183
113. PC81/265
114. R-385
115. R-2054
116. R-682
117. R-2261
118. R-681
119. R-1932
120. R-1426
121. R-1583
122. R-382
123. R-2061
124. R-619
125. R-1686
126. R-629
127. R-1704
128. R-2912
129. R-408
130. R-667
131. R-1519
132. R-1458
133. R-105
134. R-1719
135. R-1720
136. R-1278
137. R-63
138. R-1657
139. R-1673
140. R-1475
141. R-1502
142. R-580
143. R-1348
144. R-1636
145. M33-11478
146. R-2460
147. R-2405
148. R-1001
149. R-1494
150. R-17
151. R-575
152. R-1634
153. R-1635
154. R-1371

No. 155. R-391
156. R-395
157. R-2023
158. R-2001
159. M34-3773
160. R-1940
161. PC81/241
162. R-728
163. R-2021
164. PLO9B/194
165. PC81/242
166. PLO9B/245
167. R-2472
168. R-2478
169. PC81/75
170. R-2046
171. R-302
172. R-2412
173. R-2416
174. R-449
175. R-747
176. R-440
177. R-775
178. R-184
179. R-2906
180. R-724
181. R-2907
182. PC80/8
183. R-2229
184. R-215
185. R-1353
186. R-527
187. R-78
188. PC81/143
189. PLO9B/1
190. R-1381
191. R-1382
192. R-1601
193. R-208
194. PC81/67
195. PC81/254
196. J3/15
197. PC81/320
198. J3/22
199. J3/56
200. PC81/319
201. J5/49
202. H-21
203. R-1794
204. R-1238
205. J3/27
206. R-672
207. R-1225
208. R-1229
209. J5/19(207)
210. PC81/89
211. PC82/2

No. 212. PC82/3
213. PC82/5
214. PC82/8
215. PC82/12
216. PC81/128
217. PC81/234
218. PC81/129
219. J2/44
220. PC81/130
221. PC81/126
222. PC81/253
223. PC81/133
224. PC81/131
225. PC81/256
226. PC82/15
227. PC82/19
228. PC81/90
229. R-1277
230. PC82/22
231. PC81/246
232. PC81/125
233. PC81/235
234. PC82/21
235. PC81/132
236. PC82/43
237. PC82/44
238. PC81/111
239. M33-12644
240. PC81/35
241. PC81/127
242. M33-9157
243. M33-9037
243a. PC81/76
243b. PC81/280
243c. PC81/279
244. M33-9029
245. PC81/325
246. PC81/327
247. PC81/324
248. PC81/224
249. PC81/117
250. PC81/68
250a. PC81/336
250b. PC81/337
250c. PC81/338
250d. PC81/339
250e. PC81/340
250f. PC81/341
250g. PC81/342
251. PC82/25
252. M33-9102
253. PC81/196
254. PC82/24
255. H-32
256. PC82/49
257. M33-9026
258. PC81/326

No. 259. PC80/2
260. PC80/5
261. PC80/3
262. M33-9019
263. PC81/195
264. PLO2/15
265. M33-9229
266. R-1837
267. R-1174
268. PC81/287
269. PC81/286
270. PC81/263
271. PC81/121
272. PLO2/48
273. PC81/192
274. M33-9808
275. PC82/26
276. M32-9894
277. R-1776
278. M33-10040
279. M33-7897
280. PC81/16
281. R-1326
282. M33-9837
283. M33-9829
284. PC82/35
285. PC82/58
286. M33-9974
287. M33-9966
288. R-1320
289. PC81/231
290. PC82/28
291. PC81/115
292. M33-12069
293. PC81/29
294. PC81/25
295. PC81/24
296. E31820
297. E31819
298. R-1190
299. E31952
300. E31953
301. E31969
302. E31975
303. E32050
304. E32045
305. PC81/116
306. E32079
307. PC81/20
308. PC81/295
309. PLO8/36
310. M33-3476
311. R-1805
312. PC81/148
313. PC80/11
314. M33-12768
315. M34-4383

No. 316. M33-3538
317. PC81/23
318. PC81/262
319. E16717
320. PC80/9
321. PC81/248
322. R-2099
323. M31-12865A
324. R-2144
325. R-253
326. R-2177
327. PC82/31
328. PC82/30
329. R-1143
330. R-2098
331. R-2097
332. R-743
333. PC82/59
334. PC82/60
335. R-1376
336. M33-11511
337. E20769
338. M33-11503
339. M33-11505
340. M33-11495
341. M33-11563
342. M33-11570
342a. PC82/53
342b. PC82/54
342c. PC81/273
342d. PC81/274
342e. PC81/271
342f. PC81/149
342g. PC81/151
342h. PC81/278
342i. PC81/267
342j. PC81/272
342k. PC81/270
342l. PC81/269
342m. PC81/276
342n. PC81/275
342o. PC82/51
342p. PC82/52
342q. PC81/268
343. PC82/39
344. PC81/285
345. PC82/1
346. PC82/41
347. J6/33(86)
348. PC81/69
349. PC81/228
350. PC82/42
351. PC82/58
352. J4/8
353. PC81/73
354. PC82/50
355. PC82/40

No. 356. PC81/71

357. PC81/27

358. PC81/135

359. J4/12

360. PC81/70

361. PC81/255

362. PC81/245

363. PC81/142

364. PC81/318

365. R-1767

366. R-1271

367. M33-11311

368. M34-11574

369. PC81/36

370. R-1622

371. PC81/138

372. PC82/45

373. R-911

No. 374. R-1384

375. E31889

376. PC81/215

377. PC81/252

378. PC81/288

379. PC81/258

380. J4/30

381. PC81/330

382. PC81/328

383. PC82/33

384. PC81/225

385. PC81/229

386. PC81/290

387. PLO2/92

388. PC81/292

389. PC81/299

390. PC81/297

391. PC81/316

No. 392. PC81/298

393. PC81/301

394. PC81/300

395. PC81/302

396. PLO2/11

397. PLO2/1

398. PC80/6

399. PC80/7

400. PC81/201

401. PC81/303

402. PC81/304

403. PLO2/27

404. PC81/203

405. PC81/204

406. PC81/21

407. PC80/7A

408. PLO2/17

409. PC81/306

No. 410. PC81/308

411. PC81/307

412. PC81/310

413. PC81/315

414. PC81/9

415. PLO9/3

416. PC81/311

417. PC81/313

418. PC81/312

419. PC81/12

420. PC81/305

421. PC82/57

422. PC82/56

423. PC82/55

424. PC81/30

425. PC81/329

426. PC81/7

427. R-379

BEFORE
THEIR DIASPORA

was designed by Richard Zonghi, typeset in
Trump Medieval, photographed from copy prints
and printed on Monadnock Caress Colonial White Smooth
by Thomas Todd Company, Boston, and bound
in an edition of 5,000 paper cover
and 5,000 hard cover by
New Hampshire
Bindery.

DATE DUE

GAYLORD

PRINTED IN U.S.A.